United Nations Industrial Development Organization

The mandate of the United Nations Industrial Development Organization (UNIDO) is close to many of the core issues now confronting developing and transition economy countries, and this book offers the first concise and accessible guide to this important organization.

As the only UN organization to have been transformed from a UN secretariat entity to an independently governed UN agency, UNIDO is also an agency that has had to make drastic changes of focus and business practice in order to adjust to a changing environment. This book charts the complex origins and developments of the organization, and moves on to examine the current mandate of the agency, including trade capacity building, poverty reduction and the Green Industry Initiative. It also examines the significant partnerships it has formed with other UN-based systems such as the UN Conference on Trade and Development (UNCTAD) and the ITC to achieve these goals.

In the era of rapid globalization, UNIDO faces growing challenges. In the second part of this work Browne seeks to review these challenges, and UNIDO's recent reforms under its current management, and looks to suggest how the organization can help to meet some of the key global development challenges in the increasingly competitive environment of development cooperation and private-sector initiative.

This work will be a useful resource for all those with an interest in international organizations, international relations, development and trade, and international political economy.

Stephen Browne is Director of The Future of the UN Development System (FUNDS) Project and Fellow of the Ralph Bunche Institute for International Studies, The Graduate Center, City University of New York.

Routledge Global Institutions Series

Edited by Thomas G. Weiss
The CUNY Graduate Center, New York, USA
and Rorden Wilkinson
University of Manchester, UK

About the series

The Global Institutions Series has two "streams." Those with blue covers offer comprehensive, accessible, and informative guides to the history, structure, and activities of key international organizations, and introductions to topics of key importance in contemporary global governance. Recognized experts use a similar structure to address the general purpose and rationale for organizations, historical developments, membership, structure, decision-making procedures, key functions, and an annotated bibliography and guide to electronic sources. The red-cover stream consists of research monographs and edited collections that advance knowledge about one aspect of global governance; they reflect a wide variety of intellectual orientations, theoretical persuasions, and methodological approaches. Together the two streams provide a coherent and complementary portrait of the problems, prospects, and possibilities of confronting global institutions today.

Related titles in the series include:

The United Nations Development Programme and System (2011)
by Stephen Browne

The International Trade Centre (2011)
by Stephen Browne and Sam Laird

The International Labour Organization (2011)
by Steve Hughes and Nigel Haworth

The Organisation for Economic Co-operation and Development (2009)
by Richard Woodward

The International Organization for Standardization (2009)
by Craig N. Murphy and JoAnne Yates

The World Bank (2008)
by Katherine Marshall

The World Trade Organization (2007)
by Bernard M. Hoekman and Petros C. Mavroidis

UN Conference on Trade and Development (2007)
by Ian Taylor and Karen Smith

The International Monetary Fund (2007)
by James Raymond Vreeland

The World Intellectual Property Organization (2006)
by Chris May

United Nations Industrial Development Organization
Industrial solutions for a sustainable future

Stephen Browne

LONDON AND NEW YORK

First published 2012
by Routledge
2 Park Square, Milton Park, Abingdon, Oxon, OX14 4RN

Simultaneously published in the USA and Canada
by Routledge
711 Third Avenue, New York, NY 10017

Routledge is an imprint of the Taylor & Francis Group, an informa business

© 2012 Stephen Browne

The right of Stephen Browne to be identified as author of this work has been asserted by him in accordance with the Copyright, Designs and Patent Act 1988.

All rights reserved. No part of this book may be reprinted or reproduced or utilised in any form or by any electronic, mechanical, or other means, now known or hereafter invented, including photocopying and recording, or in any information storage or retrieval system, without permission in writing from the publishers.

Trademark notice: Product or corporate names may be trademarks or registered trademarks, and are used only for identification and explanation without intent to infringe.

British Library Cataloguing in Publication Data
A catalogue record for this book is available from the British Library

Library of Congress Cataloging in Publication Data
Browne, Stephen.
  United Nations Industrial Development Organization : industrial solutions for a sustainable future / Stephen Browne.
    p. cm. – (Global institutions)
  Includes bibliographical references and index.
  1. United Nations Industrial Development Organization–Handbooks, manuals, etc. I. Title.
  HC60.B7366 2012
  338.91–dc23
              2011051738

ISBN: 978-0-415-68639-6 (hbk)
ISBN: 978-0-203-11271-7 (ebk)

Typeset in Times New Roman
by Taylor & Francis Books

Contents

List of illustrations	viii
Foreword	x
Acknowledgments	xiii
List of abbreviations	xiv
Introduction: UNIDO and the role of industry in development	1
1 Origins and history of UNIDO	9
2 Current structure and mandate	30
3 Research and policy	46
4 Poverty reduction through productive activities	58
5 Penetrating global markets	88
6 Greening industry	100
7 Facing the future	125
Notes	134
Select bibliography	142
Index	146

Illustrations

Tables

2.1	UNIDO offices and representations outside Vienna	36
2.2	UNIDO expenditures by source, 1970–2010	44
2.3	UNIDO expenditures from UN multi-partner trust funds, 2004–10	45
3.1	Recent UNIDO *Industrial Development Reports*	48
6.1	Montreal Protocol: phase-out of ozone-depleting substances	102
6.2	Projections of renewable energy use in industry, 2050	114

Figures

I.1	Manufacturing value-added growth and GDP growth, 2006–10	2
2.1	UNIDO organizational structure	33
2.2	UNIDO extra-budgetary spending by source, 1972–2010	43
4.1	Industrial value-chain	61
5.1	How trade standards have evolved	90
5.2	The architecture of national quality infrastructure	93

Boxes

1.1	UNIDO objectives, 1979	14
1.2	UNIDO in Iraq	24
1.3	The United Kingdom and UNIDO	26
1.4	UNIDO milestones	27
1.5	UNIDO heads	28
2.1	UNIDO mission statement	31
2.2	Four objectives of ITPOs	38

3.1	UNIDO's Competitive Industrial Performance (CIP) index	49
4.1	Assistance to industrial clusters in Nicaragua, Ethiopia and India	69
4.2	Agro-definitions	73
4.3	UNIDO services to five agro-industrial product sectors	77
4.4	Improving the business environment in Vietnam	80
4.5	UNIDO's industrial investment appraisal tools	81
4.6	AfrIPANet	84
4.7	UNIDO and OECD's five-dimensional definition of poverty	87
5.1	Private standards and UNIDO	91
6.1	Ozone-depleting substances	101
6.2	National Cleaner Production Centres in four regions	108
6.3	Examples of cleaner production in three enterprises	111
6.4	Decoupling for sustainable economic growth	113
6.5	Sustainable Energy for All campaign, 2012–30	123

Foreword

The current volume is the 66th title in a dynamic series on global institutions. These books provide readers with definitive guides to the most visible aspects of what many of us know as "global governance." Remarkable as it may seem, there exist relatively few books that offer in-depth treatments of prominent global bodies, processes, and associated issues, much less an entire series of concise and complementary volumes. Those that do exist are either out of date, inaccessible to the non-specialist reader, or seek to develop a specialized understanding of particular aspects of an institution or process rather than offer an overall account of its functioning and situate it within the increasingly dense global institutional network. Similarly, existing books have often been written in highly technical language or have been crafted "in-house" and are notoriously self-serving and narrow.

The advent of electronic media has undoubtedly helped research and teaching by making data and primary documents of international organizations more widely available, but it has complicated matters as well. The growing reliance on the Internet and other electronic methods of finding information about key international organizations and processes has served, ironically, to limit the educational and analytical materials to which most readers have ready access—namely, books. Public relations documents, raw data, and loosely refereed websites do not make for intelligent analysis. Official publications compete with a vast amount of electronically available information, much of which is suspect because of its ideological or self-promoting slant. Paradoxically, a growing range of purportedly independent websites offering analyses of the activities of particular organizations has emerged, but one inadvertent consequence has been to frustrate access to basic, authoritative, readable, critical, and well-researched texts. The market for such has actually been reduced by the ready availability of varying quality electronic materials.

Foreword xi

For those of us who teach, research, and operate in the area, such restricted access to information and analyses has been frustrating. We were delighted when Routledge saw the value of a series that bucks this trend and provides key reference points to the most significant global institutions and issues. They are betting that serious students and professionals will want serious analyses. We have assembled a first-rate team of authors to address that market. Our intention is to provide one-stop shopping for all readers—students (both undergraduate and postgraduate), negotiators, diplomats, practitioners from non-governmental and intergovernmental organizations, and interested parties alike—seeking insights into the most prominent institutional aspects of global governance.

The United Nations Industrial Development Organization

The "correct" road to economic and social progress has been hotly contested in the corridors and conference rooms of the UN system and other world organizations. A grand institutional-ideological divide has added impetus to the long-running battle between free-market and interventionist forms of development; the result is what Jean-Philippe Thérien characterizes as "two tales of world poverty":[1] In this characterization, the hyper-liberalism of the Bretton Woods institutions, the World Bank and International Monetary Fund (IMF), and their distant cousin the World Trade Organization (WTO) has lined up against the more socially democratic institutions of the UN system in a struggle for the moral high ground in the laissez-faire versus interventionist debate. While it is certainly the case, as Thomas G. Weiss suggests, that the UN institutions have been able to soften aspects of the more fundamentalist tendencies of the Bretton Woods institutions,[2] and despite clear evidence that market intervention has been an essential element in the industrialization of *all* of the world's leading economies, the Washington Consensus (albeit a somewhat softer and power-adjusted "post" version)[3] has essentially continued to hold sway.

The UN's own specialized agency for promoting development through industrialization has been a little under the radar of the Bretton Woods versus UN system divide on how best to advance economic and social progress. Its relative obscurity, however, belies its energy in working towards improving the lives and livelihoods of the world's poorest communities. Inevitably, the story of UNIDO is bound up with grand ideological debates about how to industrialize. Equally inevitably, however, the ever-shifting flow of ideological debate has also been tempered by UNIDO's place in the "two tales of world poverty" as a UN family member and not one more closely affiliated with the ideology of the Bretton Woods institutions.

To understand UNIDO simply by its family resemblance to other development organizations in the UN system would be, however, to downplay its technical work as well as the political machinations by states during its deliberations. Moreover, such an approach would undervalue UNIDO's contributions to enhancing the lives of some of the poorest communities across the world. For these reasons alone, UNIDO is a worthy object of study. If we add in the grander ideological battles, the inclusion of a book on UNIDO in the series was a "no-brainer." It provides a fitting complement to earlier volumes on the other main actors in this arena.[4]

We are delighted that Stephen Browne agreed to write a much needed volume on this elusive but quite important institution. Stephen has over three decades of experience within the UN system, including his last position as deputy executive director of one institution that resulted in an earlier book in the series, *The International Trade Centre: Promoting Export Development* (2010). More recently, he wrote another overview for the series, *The United Nations Development Programme and System* (2011). Stephen is an unusual practitioner who found time to write while a UN official three other books on development assistance.[5] Currently he is director of The Future of the UN Development System (FUNDS) Project and Fellow of the Ralph Bunche Institute for International Studies at The Graduate Center of The City University of New York.

We are delighted to have this book in the series because it enriches the literature on global institutions and governance with a much needed title on industrial development. We wholeheartedly recommend it and, as always, welcome comments from our readers.

Thomas G. Weiss, The CUNY Graduate Center, New York, USA
Rorden Wilkinson, University of Manchester, UK
December 2011

Acknowledgments

The author benefited from a long prior acquaintance with UNIDO over many years in the field. During the writing of this book, he visited the headquarters in Vienna three times and was able to meet a large number of the staff either singly, or collectively in meetings. UNIDO makes a good habit of producing readable documentation on its activities. So, in addition to large quantities of verbal information, the author was able to hoover up a considerable amount of hard copy on the organization, supplemented with frequent visits to www.unido.org.

UNIDO's Director-General, Kandeh Yumkella provided initial inspiration for the book, the original idea for which came from Wilfried Luetkenhorst, managing director, following a conversation on the future of the UN development system. Mikhael Evstafyev, Sayaphol (Coco) Sackda, and Vinette Huber provided vital support and helped to keep the project on the rails.

A peer review team consisting of Sarwar Hobohm, Michele Clara, Kazuki Kitaoka, Cormac O'Reilly, George Assaf and Ralf Bredel undertook to review the draft and provide essential feedback. Margareta de Goys of the Evaluation Group shared her insightful and objective thoughts. Other written and verbal contributions were received from Sidi Si Ahmed, Awuor Ajwala, Ludo Alcorta, Raquel Aledo, Georgios Anestis, Bernardo Calzadilla-Sarmiento, Edward Clarence-Smith, Mahammed Dionne, Lalith Goonatilake, Chakib Jenane, Mithat Kulur, Heinz Leuenberger, Diego Masera, Gerardo Patacconi, Sergiy Prodan, Fabio Russo, Christiane Schimeck, Philippe Scholtes, Nilguen Tas, Peter Ulbrich, Igor Volodin, and Natascha Weisert

In Geneva, special thanks are due to the staff in the documents section of the UN Library in the Palais de Nations—Cristina Giordano, Carlos Adriano Gonçalves e Silva and Carla Bellota—who helped to locate historical UN texts and documents relevant to Chapter 1.

While all of the above provided valuable assistance in identifying sources and helping to correct facts and misconstructions, the author assumes full responsibility for the contents of the book and the facts and opinions within it.

Abbreviations

3ADI	African Agribusiness and Agro-industries Development Initiative
ACP	African, Caribbean and Pacific
AfDB	African Development Bank Group
AfrIPANet	Africa Investment Promotion Agency Network
AfT	Aid for Trade
AGECC	Advisory Group on Energy and Climate Change
AGOA	African Growth and Opportunity Act
AIDA	Accelerated Industrial Development of Africa
AMC	Program Approval and Monitoring Committee
AsDB	Asian Development Bank
ASEAN	Association of Southeast Asian Nations
AU	African Union
AusAID	Australian Government's overseas aid program
BIC	Business information centers
BRICS	Brazil, Russian Federation, India, China, South Africa
BWIs	Bretton Woods institutions
CAMI	Conference of African Ministers of Industry
CAP	Common Agricultural Policy
CARICOM	Caribbean Community
CCA	Common country assessment
CDA	Cluster Development Agent
CDM	Clean Development Mechanism
CEB	United Nations System Chief Executives Board for Coordination
CEMAC	Economic and Monetary Community of Central Africa
CFC	Chlorofluorocarbon
ChL	Chemical leasing

Abbreviations xv

CIP	Competitive industrial performance
COAST	Collaborative Actions for Sustainable Tourism
COMFAR	Computer Model for Feasibility Analysis and Reporting
COMPID	Combating marginalization and poverty through industrial development
CSO	Civil Society Organization
CSR	Corporate social responsibility
CSW	Commission on the Status of Women (UN)
DAC	Development Assistance Committee of the OECD
DaO	Delivering as One
DDT	Dichlorodiphenyltrichloroethane
DfID	Department for International Development
DRC	Democratic Republic of Congo
EC	European Commission
ECLAC	United Nations Economic Commission for Latin America and the Caribbean
ECOSOC	Economic and Social Council (UN)
ECOWAS	Economic Community of West African States
ECREE	ECOWAS Centre for Renewable Energy and Energy Efficiency
EIF	Enhanced Integrated Framework for Least Developed Countries
EPA	Economic partnership agreement
EU	European Union
EXIM	Export-Import Bank
FAO	Food and Agriculture Organization (UN)
FDI	Foreign direct investment
GCLME	Guinea Current Large Marine Ecosystem
GDP	Gross domestic product
GEF	Global Environment Facility
GMP	Good manufacturing practice
GNI	Gross national income
GIZ	Deutsche Gesellschaft für Internationale Zusammenarbeit (encompasses the former GTZ, Gesellschaft für Technische Zusammenarbeit)
HCFC	Hydrochlorofluorocarbon
HIV/AIDS	Human immunodeficiency virus/acquired immune deficiency syndrome
HP	Hewlett-Packard
IADB	Inter-American Development Bank
IBRD	International Bank for Reconstruction and Development (World Bank)

xvi Abbreviations

ICHET	International Centre for Hydrogen Energy Technologies
ICS	International Centre for Science and High Technology (Trieste)
I(C)T	Information (and communication) technology
IDA	International Development Association (World Bank)
IFAD	International Fund for Agricultural Development
ILO	International Labour Organization
IMF	International Monetary Fund
INEX	International Network for Educational Exchange
IPA	Investment Promotion Agency
IPS	Investment Promotion Service
IPU	Investment Promotion Unit
ISEC	International Centre for the Promotion and Transfer of Solar Energy (China)
ISO	International Organization for Standardization
ITC	International Trade Centre
ITPO	Investment and Technology Promotion Office
ITU	International Telecommunication Union
JICA	Japan International Cooperation Agency
LCOR	Leading Change and Organizational Renewal
LDC	Least Developed Country
LIFE	Learning Initiative for Entrepreneurs
MDG	Millennium Development Goal
MLA	Multilateral Mutual Recognition Agreement
MLF	Multilateral Fund (of the Montreal Protocol)
MP	Montreal Protocol on Substances that Deplete the Ozone Layer
MPI	Ministry of Planning and Investment (Vietnam)
MRA	Mutual Recognition Agreement
MSE	Micro and small enterprise
MVA	Manufacturing value added
NCPC	National Cleaner Production Center
NEPAD	New Economic Partnership for Africa
NGO	Non-governmental organization
NIEO	New international economic order
NIP	National implementation plan
Norad	Norwegian Agency for Development Cooperation
ODA	Official development assistance
ODS	Ozone-depleting substances
OECD	Organisation for Economic Co-operation and Development
OLADE	Latin American Energy Organization

OPE	Office for Project Execution (UNDP)
OPEC	Organization of Petroleum-Exporting Countries
PAC	Program Approval Committee
PCBs	Polychlorinated biphenyls
PCOR	Program for Change and Organizational Renewal
POPs	Persistent organic pollutants
PV	Photo-voltaic
REACH	Registration, Evaluation, Authorization and Restriction of Chemicals
RECP	Resource efficient and cleaner production
SAARC	South Asian Association for Regional Cooperation
SADC	Southern African Development Community
SAICM	Strategic Approach to International Chemical Management
SHP	Small hydro-power
SIDFA	Senior Industrial Development Field Advisor
SME	Small and medium-sized enterprises
SMTQ	standards, metrology, testing and quality
SPS	Sanitary and phyto-sanitary
SPX	Subcontracting and partnership exchange programme
STC	Screening and Technical Review Committee
STDF	Standards and Trade Development Facility
StEP	Solving the E-waste Problem
TA	Technical assistance
TBT	Technical Barriers to Trade
TC	Technical co-operation
TEST	Transfer of Environmentally Sound Technology
TNCs	Transnational corporations
TRIPs	Trade-Related Intellectual Property Rights
TVE	Township and village enterprises (in China)
UCSSIC	UNIDO Centre for South-South Industrial Cooperation (New Delhi)
UEMOA	West African Economic and Monetary Union
UN	United Nations
UNAIDS	Joint United Nations Programme on HIV/AIDS
UNCHAIN	University Chair on Innovation
UNCT	United Nations Country Team
UNCTC	UN Centre on Transnational Corporations
UNCTAD	United Nations Conference on Trade and Development
UNDAF	United Nations Development Assistance Framework
UNECA	United Nations Economic Commission for Africa

UNDESA	United Nations Department of Economic and Social Affairs
UNDG	United Nations Development Group
UNDP	United Nations Development Programme
UNECA	United Nations Economic Commission for Africa
UNECE	United Nations Economic Commission for Europe
UNEP	United Nations Environment Programme
UNESCAP	United Nations Economic and Social Commission for Asia and the Pacific
UNESCO	United Nations Educational, Scientific and Cultural Organization
UNFCCC	United Nations Framework Convention on Climate Change
UNFPA	United Nations Population Fund
UN-HABITAT	United Nations Human Settlements Programme
UNHCR	United Nations High Commissioner for Refugees
UNICEF	United Nations Children's Fund
UNIDO	United Nations Industrial Development Organization
UNIFEM	United Nations Development Fund for Women
UNODC	UN Office for Drugs and Crime
UNU	United Nations University
UNU-MERIT	UN University Maastricht Economic and Social Research Institute of Innovation and Technology
UNU-WIDER	UN University World Institute for Development Economics Research
UNWTO	World Tourism Organization
VIC	Vienna International Centre
WFP	World Food Programme (UN)
WHO	World Health Organization (UN)
WIPO	World Intellectual Property Organization (UN)
WMO	World Meteorological Organization (UN)
WTO	World Trade Organization

Introduction
UNIDO and the role of industry in development

The United Nations Industrial Development Organization (UNIDO) was created as the UN development system's focal point and coordinator for activities of industrial promotion. The importance of industrialization to economic growth and development—signified by the fact that the term "industrialized" is used synonymously with advanced development—had long been acknowledged. The emergence of an industrial development organization in the international public sector, therefore, might have seemed uncontroversial. However, the ideological rivalries instilled by Cold War politics, and the doubts in a few influential developed countries about the role of the public sector in industrial promotion, surrounded UNIDO in controversy from its earliest days. Its emergence as a full-fledged specialized agency of the UN system was, mainly in consequence, belabored in spite of strong and unwavering support from the overwhelming majority of developing countries, a juxtaposition of power and influence which has accompanied many UN and other multilateral agencies.[1]

Thus there are two fundamental questions underlying the UNIDO story and an account of its fortunes. What is the evidence for the importance of industrialization (which encompasses manufacturing and basic processing of raw materials)? Why specifically has the role of the public sector in the process of industrialization been perceived as controversial?

Empirical evidence of the dynamic role of industrialization—and the manufacturing and processing sector in particular—is not hard to find, and has been charted by UNIDO over the years. Figure I.1 shows the close association between manufacturing value added (MVA)[2] and the growth in gross domestic product (GDP) for 157 developing countries in recent years. For earlier periods, the pattern is the same. A correlation does not determine causation, of course, but growth and development are structural processes, typically involving the movement of labor from agriculture to manufacturing, and thence to services. As labor moves

2 Introduction

out of farming and into processing and manufacturing, productivity and incomes rise. The faster this economic migration occurs, the faster the rate of economic growth. The pattern is not invariable. However, there are few exceptions to development along a path from primary-to-secondary sector transformation, which has been the pattern from the eighteenth-century English industrial revolution onwards.

The most spectacular examples of industry-led growth have come from East Asia. The way was pioneered by Japan. The first four "flying geese"[3] (or Asian Tigers as they came to be known) followed a somewhat similar pattern: South Korea, Chinese Taipei (Taiwan), Singapore and Hong Kong. The last two were unusual in that they started as very small enclave economies with almost no agriculture, but they favored industrial growth with high savings and dynamic exports to developed markets. Hong Kong and Singapore also relied on high levels of foreign direct investment (FDI). Accelerated industrialization was no accident. Individual sectors were targeted and favored with fiscal and trade incentives and state-administered financial institutions irrigated their growth with capital. Other factors helping to sustain the expansion were investment in education and, arguably, cultural conditions which—along with authoritarian government—were conducive to a relatively quiescent and adaptable labor force. These four economies consistently achieved annual growth of between 8 percent and 10 percent.[4]

A second group of Asian economies was the next to take flight. From the 1970s, Indonesia, Malaysia, and Thailand emulated key aspects of the East Asian experience and achieved high and sustained growth.[5] These

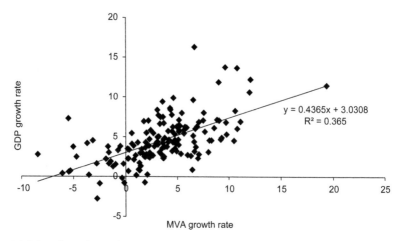

I.1 Manufacturing value-added growth and GDP growth, 2006–10

countries also reached high levels of literacy, raised domestic savings levels and actively courted foreign investment. In contrast to the tigers, their early development was heavily reliant on their rich natural resource base. Each also had substantial agriculture and fisheries sectors which, in the case of Malaysia and Thailand, supported a first phase of export-led growth. What is important to note, however, is that these countries, although very generously endowed with a wide range of minerals, fisheries and cash crops, built their high and sustained growth on an industrial base.

At the end of the 1970s, China also awoke to the potential of industrialization. Under the same combination of an authoritarian state committed to education, and a thrifty and entrepreneurial labor force, "township and village enterprises" (TVEs) were allowed to operate with a rising degree of commercial freedom, although not initially privately owned. TVEs were a special case of the transformation from agriculture to industry, since most were located in rural areas and helped to supplement farmers' incomes. The TVEs underwent major changes in the 1990s, but the eventual impact of these new manufacturing enterprises on some villages was nothing short of spectacular. An often-cited example is Qiaotou, which grew from a rural settlement in the 1980s to become the center of production of two-thirds of the world's entire output of buttons.[6]

By the first decade of the millennium, MVA for all of these Asian flying geese economies was 25 percent of GDP or more (with the exception of Hong Kong which had by then transformed itself further to become almost exclusively a service economy). At around 35 percent, China and Thailand had the highest level of any economies in the world. In other developing regions, individual countries have also enjoyed rapid growth although their manufacturing sectors did not reach the same relative levels. Among low-income economies, these include Egypt and India, and among upper- and middle-income economies, Botswana, Chile and Tunisia. India's growth was also based on expansion of services, and Chile's on agriculture. However, in every case growth of MVA per capita and MVA per worker—a measure of manufacturing productivity—has been higher, in some cases significantly, than among slow-growing countries.

The performance of East Asia and the dynamic economies in other regions demonstrates that increasing industrialization is a spur to economic expansion, and that large manufacturing sectors help to sustain growth. The sustained success of the East Asian economies also contains lessons about patterns of industrialization. The contrast with Latin America is instructive. Between 1965 and 1980, while East Asia's manufacturing sector grew proportionately by 10 percentage points, Latin America's remained the same relative size and then subsequently shrank.[7] Two of the major differences between the regions were that Asia succeeded in building a more broadly based manufacturing sector and achieved larger increases in productivity, thus ensuring greater competitiveness. In fact, the composition of the manufacturing sector is an important determinant of the effectiveness of industrialization in spurring overall economic growth.

UNIDO research confirms that, whatever the income levels of developing countries, the more diversified is manufacturing and the more technologically complex (or "sophisticated") are the production processes, the greater the contribution to growth. These conclusions are intuitively appealing. More diverse economies are more flexible and responsive. A wider range of manufacturing activities facilitates the entry and exit of enterprises and enables countries to take more advantage of new marketing opportunities as they arise.[8]

The advance of globalization through improved international communications and transport, and lower trade barriers, has provided new opportunities for developing countries to export niche products from the farm, as well as footloose services in information technology and business process outsourcing. However, access to global markets has raised the premium highest on manufacturing, of which some developing countries have taken full advantage, allowing them to grow at historically unprecedented rates. Thus, external trade has become critical to industrialization; indeed, the planetary scale of manufacturing is a mainstay of the globalization process. For countries with small domestic economies, global markets provide almost limitless demand for their manufactured goods. These need not be finished products, since a substantial proportion of trade is in intermediate goods, often internal to major global corporations. The automobile industry is a prime example. More and more developing countries are thus trading in "tasks," i.e. stages in a global production process, which accounts for a growing proportion of global commerce. UNIDO estimates that "imported intermediates" constituted 12 percent of total global manufacturing output during the period 1986–90 and 18 percent by 2000. Growing reliance on imported intermediates is a feature of manufacturing in all regions.[9]

The example of the dynamic East Asian economies, and the opportunities offered by globalization, are the basis for a substantial agenda for an industrial promotion organization like UNIDO. As the organization's own analysis confirms, even those it terms the "least developed manufacturing countries" with small domestic markets can discover

Introduction 5

niche markets or enter global value chains by trading in tasks. Through industrialization, moreover, it is not merely growth that is stimulated. New manufacturing activities generate jobs and incomes in cities as well as in rural areas, as the Chinese example has shown.

Now comes the second question. These examples of successful industrialization only become an "agenda" if public bodies like UNIDO at the global level, and governments at the national level are perceived as playing an instrumental role. This is where the debate becomes controversial.

From the 1980s, the development paradigm was dominated by neoliberal thinking which advocated minimal economic intervention. The advice emanating from institutions such as the World Bank and International Monetary Fund (IMF) was critical of industrial policy as an inappropriate way to "pick winners" and then favor them through subsidies and tax incentives. Macro-economic stability and free markets constituted the prevailing gospel of the Washington consensus, with minimal interference from the state. According to this orthodoxy, the example of East Asia was touted as exceptional and unique to their cultural and political traditions. When the 1997–98 crisis hit the Asian economies and brought their expansion to a halt, industrial policy was blamed as one of the causes.

These non-interventionist arguments were used by some developed country governments to question the rationale for an international public organization like UNIDO, which itself characterized these objections as follows: "Was a publicly-funded body still needed to support industrial development in the new global economy, characterized by widespread liberalization, the primacy of market forces, and the leading role of the private sector in development?"[10]

Practice provided an answer: industrialization could be fostered with the right kinds of guidance. By the new millennium, it had become clear that the orthodox development prescriptions were not working. The prevailing economic thinking was blamed for neglecting the importance of "structural transformation and industrial development," in spite of the empirical evidence of the benefits.[11] Then the financial meltdown in many of the developed economies in 2007–08 was a dramatic demonstration of deregulation gone awry. In pleading for a "new industrial policy," UNIDO itself pointed out in its journal *Making It*: "it has taken a major global economic crisis to drive home the point that markets are all about allocation of resources and efficiency but, in and by themselves, they do not take care of long-term societal objectives."[12] In responding to the crisis, the developed countries, whose governments had been advising developing countries against intervention, indulged in their own major programs of intervention. Governments mounted bail-outs of the automobile and other industries and applied targeted subsidies as part of huge stimulus packages. In a sign that industrial policy was back in vogue, the Commission of the 27-country European Union (EU) published *An Integrated Industrial Policy for the Globalization Era* in October 2010. Developing countries could legitimately complain of double standards.[13] Today there is still dogmatic reasoning on both sides of the debate, but the case for industrial policy can more confidently be made.

In reaction to the second question, therefore, the challenge for UNIDO is to know how and what policies to apply to those countries that are still substantially pre-industrial and low-income. In many cases, e.g. in Africa, countries have devised industrial policies, but with limited success. The pattern of industrial policy in Africa initially followed import substitution, with governments attempting to channel investment into domestic activities for which there appeared to be a ready market. Many countries took a statist approach, maintaining key industrial activities under public ownership and manipulating the costs of capital, import tariffs and fiscal regimes in favor of domestic production. By the late 1970s, however, manufacturing growth had slowed to zero or even negative growth in some economies.[14] The contemporary case for industrial policy in Africa and other non-industrialized countries, therefore, must eschew the mistakes of the past.

With the renewed interest in industrial policy and its importance, but taking account of the lessons of experience, new patterns of industrial policy have been advocated by Dani Rodrik and others.[15] This process of reinvention is analogous to new theories of trade.[16] These new theories get away from traditional arguments about factor endowments and emphasize how development can be proactively encouraged through productive partnerships between the public and private sectors. Private sectors should lead and governments should support, and part of that support consists of compensating for some of the imperfections of markets.

"New" policies encourage the search for innovation, rather than protecting established industries, embracing the discovery process mentioned above. As UNIDO puts it, this search is "organized as a collaborative public-private process of learning with manifold feedback loops; it helps to speed up market processes and builds on customer-oriented and business-like service providers."[17] Importantly, policy should not be standardized and prescriptive, but specifically tailored to the circumstances of each country. Industrial policy does not seek to produce blueprints, but concentrates on learning through experimentation and on the adaptation of promising approaches to local contexts. These

Introduction 7

new policies have provided a model, which UNIDO has sought to follow in its own work.

To sum up so far, the rationale for a public body like UNIDO is founded, first, on very strong evidence from post-war experience of the importance of industrialization in driving the development process, and second, on the advocacy and propagation of appropriate industrial policies by governments.

A third rationale would be the new policy imperatives impelled by climate change. UNIDO has called environmental deterioration "a result of the greatest market failure the world has seen,"[18] and it may provide the strongest justification yet for public intervention in industrialization processes which, by some estimates, account for more than one-third of global CO_2 emissions. Addressing the environmental hazards associated with industry is a huge challenge, but is amenable to solution. In a very real sense, international cooperation through the UN has already saved the planet once. In 1985, arguably the most successful international agreement in the sphere of development was concluded in Vienna: the Convention on the Protection of the Ozone Layer. The convention was drawn up in response to a serious depletion of ozone in the earth's atmosphere which threatened human and animal health through increased ultra-violet radiation. The cause was the emission of chlorofluorocarbons (CFCs) and other ozone-depleting substances (ODS) by numerous industrial processes, and it led in 1987 to the Montreal Protocol which set targets for steep cuts in CFCs.

UNIDO has been ideally placed to assist countries to meet their obligations under Montreal and reduce ODSs by revamping their industrial processes. The much broader ongoing concerns about climate change call for renewed efforts to "green industry," suggesting a substantial augmentation of UNIDO's responsibilities.

This book tells the UNIDO story from its earliest beginnings as a modest unit in the UN secretariat in New York to a full-fledged specialized agency in Vienna (Chapter 1). The chapter traces the ideological objections from some developed countries which slowed the emergence of the organization. It tracks the periodic funding difficulties and managerial challenges that it faced, and its subsequent reform and revival over the last decade. UNIDO has remained true to the original vocation enshrined in its constitution, which describes its dual role as a global forum for industrial debate, and as purveyor of technical assistance.

Chapter 2 describes the organization as it is today: its new mission statement, a more streamlined structure, its field presence, programming practices, governance arrangements, and the many partnerships that it has forged with other organizations within and beyond the UN system. The chapter concludes with a review of the current funding situation.

Chapter 3 describes the brain at the centre of UNIDO which has maintained its data-gathering and research activities, developed its analytical tools and advanced the organization's thinking on industrial policy. These are the activities underpinning its first role as a global forum. The arguments on both sides of the policy debate are found here, as well as the main elements of "new" industrial policy, which has helped to bring a more interventionist role of the state back into vogue.

Chapters 4, 5, and 6 are about UNIDO's second role of technical assistance provider. The organization currently divides its activities into three priority areas. The first is the more traditional one of building productive capacity, the subject of Chapter 4. The chapter describes the wide range of different, not to say quite disparate, activities designed to strengthen the productive and competitive capacities of (mainly) small enterprises as a means of reducing poverty. UNIDO's record as poverty-reducer is also reviewed.

Chapter 5 is mainly about helping countries to improve what it calls their "quality infrastructure." UNIDO does not set industrial standards but it has long been active in helping enterprises in developing countries to meet them. Product quality becomes of paramount importance as these enterprises seek to penetrate increasingly open global markets, which has given a distinct trade spin to these activities. With the advent of more "aid for trade," UNIDO sees growing opportunities to expand its activities in this area.

Chapter 6 describes UNIDO's work in "greening" industry. As mentioned above, helping countries to adhere to the Montreal Protocol was tailor-made for the competences of UNIDO, and it has expanded its reach into environmental concerns encompassing all aspects of cleaner production, including energy efficiency, and effluent and waste reduction and disposal.

The final chapter takes stock of the organization and assesses its prospects. It faces the imminent withdrawal of another major donor country, recalling the ideological debate of an earlier period. However, with continuing reform and adjustment, there are opportunities for UNIDO to align itself around a "quality" agenda and pursue new ways of connecting with its partners and clients.

1 Origins and history of UNIDO

- Hesitant beginnings
- New status
- Funding crisis
- UNIDO under fire
- A new reform phase
- Conclusion

No part of the United Nations (UN) development system has evolved through as many stages as the UN Industrial Development Organization (UNIDO), which is what makes its origins and history of special interest. The organization—growing from a modest UN division to a full-fledged specialized agency—has undergone considerable buffeting along the way, in part a reflection of the doubts of the dominant developed country donors about the proper place of an international public agency in the promotion of industrial development. This chapter traces UNIDO's evolution that accompanied these concerns. This book will return to address the question of role more fully in the final chapter.

Like many other UN entities, UNIDO has been the victim of funding vagaries. The uncertainties were exacerbated when its principal source of technical assistance (TA) funding within the UN withdrew its support for reasons that had little to do with performance. Consequently, UNIDO became even more dependent on bilateral donors and right up until the present day, it has been preoccupied with staying onside with its principal patrons.

A funding nadir was reached in the 1990s, and UNIDO had to weather further criticism from developed countries, some of which subsequently withdrew from the organization. However, it managed to build back better. It cut down drastically on redundant activities and concentrated its growth on areas of emerging priority, including trade capacity building and the promotion of production processes more sustainable in terms of energy and the environment. Today, the organization has regained its earlier levels of activity, with substantially fewer staff.

Hesitant beginnings

In the post-war debates within the UN on economic and social issues, industrial development was a relative latecomer to the agenda. For its first 10 years, the UN was preoccupied with financing, trade, transport and a range of social questions including full employment, the status of women and children, refugees, narcotic drugs, social welfare and human rights.[1]

From 1952, however, the Economic and Social Council (ECOSOC) began asking for studies on productivity, and two years later the secretariat produced a working paper, *Efforts Towards Raising Productivity in Industry*.[2] It mainly consisted of a review of the findings of technical assistance missions on the state of manufacturing in the "under-developed countries." Further work was requested and at the end of 1954 a much more substantial and erudite report was published: *Process and Problems of Industrialization in Under-Developed Countries*.[3] One of its principal authors was Hans Singer, the senior economist in the secretariat at the time, and those contributing to the final draft included some of the best development minds of the day: Barbara Ward, Arthur Lewis, Simon Kuznets, Dennis Robertson, and Jan Tinbergen. A section of the report considered the implications for international organizations, noting that at the time of publication, very limited assistance had been provided to "secondary industry." The World Bank—concentrating much more heavily on infrastructure—had extended only two loans (to India and Yugoslavia), while only 5 percent of UN technical assistance had been directed at manufacturing and mining.[4] The paucity of funds allocated for industrial development was attributed to two factors, which corroborate the relatively low priority put on industrial development by governments:

> In the first place, countries in the pre-industrial phase of development are seldom in a position to take full advantage of aid in this field ... In the second place, in many under-developed areas where secondary industry has been established, it is largely in the hands of private entrepreneurs and therefore lies outside the direct range of aid provided to governments.[5]

Kick-starting industrialization and supporting the private sector are both concerns that would have to be answered by any forms of international public assistance to the secondary sector.

From 1956, the UN drew up a program of work in industrialization and an industry section was established in the secretariat to undertake and coordinate the UN's work in this domain. This was the first seed from which UNIDO was eventually to grow. Three years later, the section became a full branch. In 1961 a committee for industrial development met for the first time under the auspices of ECOSOC and recommended the creation of an industrial development center within the secretariat, which began formally the following year. In the General Assembly debate later in that year, the idea of a specialized agency was mooted for the first time, and supported and opposed by an almost equal number of countries.

Momentum continued to grow, however. In 1964 the first UN Conference on Trade and Development called for the eventual creation of a specialized agency. The following year the General Assembly passed a resolution setting up an organization for industrial development[6] and in 1966—acting on a recommendation of an *ad hoc* committee—the General Assembly approved the creation of UNIDO as an "autonomous organization within the United Nations."[7] By the same resolution, it was decided to establish an industrial development board as UNIDO's principal organ (replacing the committee for industrial development), comprising 45 members drawn from four different country groups (Latin America and Caribbean, other developing, centrally planned and industrialized countries). Financing of administrative costs and research would come from the regular budget of the UN, while operational activities would be supported by voluntary contributions and UN Development Programme (UNDP) funding.[8] In December 1966, having considered several offers of host facilities, the General Assembly decided to locate UNIDO in Vienna. In January 1967 UNIDO opened for business in its new European home.[9]

The creation of UNIDO as an autonomous UN body was something of a compromise.[10] The developing countries, which now comprised a large majority of the UN membership, wanted a specialized agency with its own governing body, while the developed countries preferred an organization with more modest ambitions under the auspices of the General Assembly. This tension, which has been intrinsic to the UN development system throughout its history, was the result of a fundamental incongruity in development cooperation. Unlike in the pre-war era, the countries requesting technical services were not required to pay for them. Not being the principal paymasters of the system, they therefore did not exercise ultimate control over the UN organizations, and could not even guarantee that their demands would be met. This incongruity has always been taken for granted in the aid sphere.

In their bilateral programs, the donor countries have largely dictated the direction and nature of their aid. However, the multilateral system, too, has been dominated by the interests of the major donors—a tendency that has only become more marked with time as earmarked financing has become predominant. As this history will soon reveal, a dependence on financing from a limited number of major donors was to render the UN development system—and UNIDO in particular—vulnerable to the funding policies of a limited number of governments, the accountability of which is primarily to rich taxpayers in the North rather than poor beneficiaries in the South.

To start with, UNIDO's activities continued those of the former centre for industrial development. It acted as a global forum for discussions, undertook research and analysis and disseminated information. Donors had decreed that technical assistance ("operational activities") should be financed from "extra-budgetary" sources. Over its first full decade UNIDO's resources grew four times. In 1970 its total budget was almost US$32 million, of which extra-budgetary resources accounted for $20 million. By 1980, resources had grown to $123 million, of which nearly $73 million were from extra-budgetary sources, mainly UNDP (see Table 2.2 in Chapter 2).

During 1972 and 1973 a group of 18 "high-level experts" established by the UN Secretary-General deliberated on a long-range strategy for UNIDO. Their report was then considered, and substantially endorsed the following year, by an *ad hoc* committee comprising representatives of 27 countries, which the Industrial Development Board set up for the purpose. Its recommendations pertained to the role and scope of UNIDO and urged greater financial and administrative autonomy.

The decade of the 1970s was marked by strident debate about what was perceived by developing countries as a highly inequitable global economy. The terms of trade had continued to move against the exporters of primary goods, yet market access into the developed countries was limited by tariffs that escalated with higher degrees of processing and manufacture. Rich country protectionism was compounded by opaque non-tariff measures and the persistence of agricultural subsidies for the benefit of an affluent and rapidly diminishing farming population. The terms of international finance were also dictated by the rich countries while their multinational corporations dominated the international flows of private capital and technology.

In 1973 the developing country oil-exporters held back on supply and ramped up the price of petroleum in a graphic manifestation of commodity cartelism. For developing countries the Organization of Petroleum Exporting Countries (OPEC) provided an example that they sought to emulate and, encouraged by their intergovernmental pressure group—known as the G-77—they began to make demands on the rich world for a "new international economic order." At a special session in 1974, the General Assembly passed resolutions on the Declaration and Programme of Action on the Establishment of a New International Economic Order (NIEO)[11] designed, no less, to transform the structure of economic relations.

There was more rhetoric than result.[12] The UN Conference on Trade and Development (UNCTAD) began a protracted campaign to establish a common fund as defense against continuing real declines in exported non-oil commodities. Agreement was finally reached only in 1980, but it was another nine years before the fund became a reality. The developed countries made modest concessions on trade and debt relief, and donor aid flows accelerated in the second half of the decade, but there was little fundamental change, and the developed countries continued to dominate the main international organs of economic power which had been created to redress global imbalances: the World Bank, International Monetary Fund (IMF) and the General Agreement on Tariffs and Trade (GATT).[13] The unfortunate long-term consequences of the NIEO's failure were that, by maintaining an unequal balance in the global economy, the rich countries had a rationale for continuing patronage in the form of aid, while the developing countries were provided with external scapegoats for their lack of development progress.

Against the backdrop of the NIEO, UNIDO held its second general conference in 1975 in Peru. It resulted in the Lima Declaration and Plan of Action on Industrial Development and Cooperation.[14] Lima was couched in the language of the global debate. It called for the share of the developing countries in world industrial production to be raised from the prevailing 7 percent to 25 percent by 2000,[15] and for special measures to assist the least developed, land-locked and island developing countries. UNIDO was seen by developing countries as a key actor in implementing the NIEO Declaration, and this was the origin of the "global forum" role envisaged for the organization.[16] The global forum was to be the venue for a "system of consultations" in order to "facilitate the establishment of a new international economic order"—in effect, an industrial pressure group for the South. Lima also called for developed countries to:

> ... undertake an objective and critical examination of their present policies and make appropriate changes in such policies so as to facilitate the expansion and diversification of imports from developing

countries and thereby make possible international economic relations on a rational, just and equitable basis.[17]

UNIDO was perceived by some as attaining a status equivalent to the Bretton Woods Institutions,[18] but with a more equitable (UN-style) governance structure. Behind the labored style and the awkward nuances of inter-governmental debate, Lima echoed the rhetoric of the new international economic order in calling for a rebalancing of global economic power. It was idealistic declamation typical of the era, but as UNIDO's newly appointed executive director (formerly with OPEC) put it at the time, "the ill-assorted but still encircling armaments of the third world were in opposition to the firm and controlled resistance of the industrialized countries ... the instruments to be mobilized and the measures to be implemented belonged exclusively to the developed countries."[19] Action was never likely to follow words as long as developing countries without oil were unable to exercise economic leverage. What Lima did, however, was to establish UNIDO as the industrial equivalent of UNCTAD, which was for a time the principal mouthpiece of the developing world in trade matters.

The North–South divide also underlay UNIDO's future course as an institution: its constitution enshrined the NIEO in its first article (see Box 1.1). Developing countries wanted its autonomy to be increased and its ambition reaffirmed as a future UN specialized agency. Following Lima, the UN Secretary-General initiated the preparation of a constitution, for which an "intergovernmental committee" was established. The draft was scrutinized by sessions of a special UN conference and approved in April 1979, following which it was open for signature. However, to enter into force, the constitution had to be ratified by a minimum of 80 member states and they had to include a sufficient number of developed countries to ensure a secure funding base.

Box 1.1 UNIDO objectives, 1979

The Constitution of UNIDO, April 1979, Article 1, states that "the primary objective of the Organization shall be the promotion and acceleration of industrial development in the developing countries with a view to assisting in the establishment of a new international economic order. The Organization shall also promote industrial development and cooperation on global, regional and national, as well as on sectoral levels."

In practice, the organization exercises four broad functions: technical assistance (or technical cooperation), "global forum" through the convening of meetings, policy and research, and a normative role, which mainly entails assisting countries and enterprises to meet internationally determined standards.

Some developed countries remained skeptical of the need for a new UN specialized agency. The funding obligation that went with a new assessed budget—in addition to that of the UN organization which had supported UNIDO from the beginning—was just one of the issues. The major donor countries also had misgivings about an organization that could create competitors by assisting the private manufacturers of developing countries. More constructively, they were concerned about lack of coordination within the UN system.[20] These concerns delayed the ratification process for several years until 1985, and it was not until 1 January of the following year that UNIDO formally became a UN specialized agency. The journey from Lima had taken a full 10 years.

New status

The formalization of UNIDO's status as a UN specialized agency would seem to have given belated recognition to the significance of industrial development and the key role that UNIDO could play in promoting it. Amongst the staff there was heady enthusiasm about the future of the organization. The optimism was tempered, however, by an early funding crisis. The first biennial budget came up 30 percent short as governments proved to be slow or reluctant contributors. The situation was made worse by a decline in the value of the dollar against the Austrian Schilling, in which most of the costs were paid. (It would have been an opportunity to move to a Schilling- (now euro-) based budget, like UNIDO's UN neighbor in Vienna the International Atomic Energy Agency (IAEA). However, this move was opposed by the organization's then director of finance.)

The financial crisis was a major distraction for UNIDO's first director-general (DG) in the new era, Domingo L. Siazon of the Philippines. His managerial space was further cramped by pressures from member states for representation in high-level posts—a balancing task made more complex by the need imposed by the board to appoint five deputy directors-general (at UN assistant secretary-general level), when the DG would have preferred one.[21]

From 1987, however, although substantial assessed contributions to the regular budget were still outstanding, the hitherto stagnant non-core funding for technical assistance grew rapidly, in large part as the financial fortunes of the main source, UNDP, revived. From less than $100 million in 1985, UNIDO delivered assistance worth almost $160 million in 1990, compared with $95.9 million for headquarters expenditures. From a total of 976 in 1976, the number of staff in Vienna had grown in 1990 to 1,392 (of whom 458 professionals), with a further 39 country directors serving in the field.

After five years UNIDO's new status seemed to be fully justified by its rapid expansion; total spending grew by over 70 percent between 1985 and 1990. However, the climate was about to change rather suddenly and brutally, with painful repercussions for UNIDO.

Funding crisis

After 1990, funds for technical assistance began to fall off sharply. The main reason for the initial decline was a fall in funding from UNDP, which had been the principal source for projects since UNIDO's inception. The circumstances of the UNDP withdrawal were unfortunate. UNDP had been specifically established in 1965 as a central TA fund for the whole UN development system, comprising the 30 or so organizations and agencies concerned with longer-term development. However, UNDP's role as a central funder and coordinator had never been effective, both because of the overall inadequacy of UNDP resources and because of the inclination of each part of the system to enhance its own independence. UNIDO's accession to specialized agency status was one manifestation, but UNDP itself also sought to become a development organization in its own right, downplaying its coordination role.

From the early part of the decade, UNDP began channeling its funding away from the rest of the system. One reason was that UNDP wanted to shift resources into other development domains which did not correspond with the sectoral orientation of the agencies. Industrial development fell out of favor, although UNDP continued to fund projects that fell into the domains of other UN organizations and agencies. Also, rather than relying on implementing agencies as intermediaries between funder and beneficiary, UNDP wanted to increase more direct "national execution," even though this appeared to the agencies to result in more "self-execution" through UNDP's own Office for Project Execution (OPE). A business reason for excluding the agencies was to help speed up the process of identifying and approving projects which under the traditional tripartite process (governments, agencies, UNDP) was often cumbersome. However, this also resulted in UNDP spending more TA funds on itself, either through OPE or through programs and staff that it managed directly.[22] Developing country governments willingly endorsed these forms of more direct implementation, but as a result the specialized expertise that resided in the rest of the UN system was excluded.

UNDP funding of UNIDO's TA fell in every year after 1990. Although UNIDO came to call on other sources, the total value of its project delivery was almost halved by 1996. The Industrial Development Fund had been created in 1979 and this had been intended to become the principal source of TA. Target annual funding was $50 million but pledges never exceeded $30 million in any one year. In the early stages, many of the major donors considered that UNDP would be a more appropriate source, but they did not take up the slack when UNDP funding tailed off. The fall in TA resources would have been greater but for the creation of the multilateral fund of the Montreal Protocol, a facility set up to assist countries to reduce the use and emissions of ozone-depleting substances from their manufacturing industries. UNIDO was an obvious beneficiary of this fund which is one of the principal reasons why the organization has taken on important new environmental responsibilities (see Chapter 6).

Globally, there were other important changes influencing technical assistance. The reunification of Germany in 1989 and the break-up of the Soviet Union in 1991 amounted to both an ideological and a practical watershed. Ideologically, market-driven democracy became the universal paradigm of development. The role of the state was changing from the management of industry to facilitation, and whereas the concerns of state-managed industry had been an important focus of UNIDO's activities in newly independent developing countries in its early years, there was now a preoccupation with the less familiar areas of economic liberalization and privatization, requiring new skills and approaches. At the same time, the manufacturing sectors in the countries of Eastern Europe and the former Soviet Union were facing critical problems of survival as their traditional sources and markets dried up. The new political realities thus posed additional challenges for UNIDO to meet with limited resources.

The end of the Cold War also led to declining foreign aid linked to geo-politics. An unfavorable economic conjuncture in the developed countries encouraged budget stringencies which, in Europe, were compounded by the need for fiscal alignment prior to the introduction of the single currency. Between 1992 and 1997 official development assistance from the Organisation for Economic Co-operation and Development (OECD) countries fell by almost 30 percent in real terms, leading to cutbacks in the funding of multilateral institutions including UNIDO.

UNIDO under fire

Internally, all was not well. In 1991 a special advisory group to the director-general was set up, which highlighted some of the organizational weaknesses of UNIDO, including a lack of focus and poor project preparation. Recognizing the challenges facing the organization both from outside and from within, the following year the Danish Government sponsored a study of "the comparative advantages, areas of concentration, organization and resources" of UNIDO.[23] The study was intended as "a contribution to the debate on making UNIDO a more efficient and effective organization"[24] and it provided a useful diagnosis. UNIDO should concentrate on providing assistance at three "target levels": the policy and strategic level, the institutional framework level and the enterprise level. In doing so, said the report, it should build on four areas of comparative advantage: its relationship with governments which facilitated policy dialogue; a readiness to recognize the linkages among the three levels of intervention; specialized knowledge of some industrial operations; and a capacity to analyze experience of industrial development from all parts of the world.

Partly inspired by the Danish study, the UNIDO secretariat embarked on a major reform program which a new director-general, Mauricio de Maria y Campos, took to the fifth general conference held in Yaoundé, Cameroon, in December 1993. The program was approved and from 1994, implementation began. Then UNIDO's crisis deepened further. The consultations that had preceded the reform program had clearly not stemmed the criticism of some of the key donor governments. At the beginning of 1995 the Commission on Global Governance—set up as a sequel to the 1991 Stockholm Initiative on global security and governance and comprising 26 renowned experts from both North and South—completed its report. Among its recommendations was the closure of both UNIDO and UNCTAD.

In UNIDO's case, the reasoning was that most developing countries:

> ... have established a wide range of industries, accumulating considerable experience both in industrial promotion and negotiations with trans-national corporations. A number of other agencies have also emerged as sources of technical assistance in those fields. Overall, industrial development is no longer viewed as a unique solution to the economic development of developing countries.[25]

The logic is curious. While experience counts for a lot, many developing countries had not, by the mid-1990s, successfully translated "industrial promotion" into sustainable industrialization, which remains—as seen in the Introduction—the main engine of economic growth in most poor countries.

However, damage had been done. An influential report had for the first time called for a shrinking and consolidation of the UN development system and several donor governments—which had already expressed their concerns about UNIDO—appeared sympathetic. In 1994 Canada had already withdrawn from the organization and the largest donor, the United States, followed in 1995. The United States' withdrawal was a severe blow. Not only did it mean a cut of 25 percent in the regular budget but the United States also left with substantial arrears—amounting to $61 million—in transgression of the terms of the constitution.[26] These withdrawals (followed by Australia in 1997, with threats to withdraw coming from Germany, the United Kingdom and others) greatly heightened the sense of urgency.

During the period 1994–97, budget stringency brought some swingeing changes. Total staff numbers fell by over 40 percent to 755. Among the posts abolished were the five deputy directors-general (none of which was ever restored). With the heaviest staff cuts falling on administration, some services were contracted out, overhead costs were cut and a number of internal procedures were modernized and streamlined. By 1997, the secretariat structure was flatter and more focused. The three target sectors (each with many sub-sectors) were agro-based industries, chemicals and engineering, and in addition there were seven non-sectoral themes.

Yet UNIDO was still not out of crisis. These reforms were not sufficient to convince all the larger donors to support the organization, in spite of a growing demand for its services. Donor concerns were deep-seated. Since the 1970s, UNIDO had become closely identified with the aspirations of the developing world. As in UNCTAD forums, these aspirations had taken on political dimensions, leading to justifiable demands not just for transfers of assistance, but for a rebalancing of an inequitable global economy. However, as a former UNIDO executive director (cited above) had pointed out, little was likely to change if all the cards were being held by the North. Experience has shown that fundamental change in the world economy has usually occurred only when the developing countries are able to summon up countervailing strengths, whether oil embargoes in the 1970s or, more recently, the development of highly competitive exports.[27] In a globalizing world especially, commercial might is right.

Thus, while idealistically the multilateral system might have been conceived as a means of helping to permanently rebalance global inequalities, in practice it has been used mainly as a conduit for assistance from North to South. As long as the system has been heavily dependent on funding from the developed countries, they have expected to continue driving the agendas of the multilateral organizations. Where those expectations are not met, donor interest diminishes. So it has proved with UNIDO, caught up in a broader crisis of multilateralism. From 1997, the organization had no choice but to respond to the continuing criticism of the developed countries if it was to sustain their financial support, particularly in the light of the withdrawal of several members.

A new reform phase

Denmark—always critical but constructive in its attitude to UNIDO—again showed its readiness to assist the reform process. Five years on from *A Future UNIDO*, the Danish Government sponsored a second and more comprehensive review which was completed in May 1997.[28] The authors of the report admitted to a "not particularly positive" impression of UNIDO's effectiveness at the start of their review. However, following their work, they determined that some of the criticism was unwarranted and that the secretariat "had managed to improve its overall performance considerably within a few years,"[29] justifying the continued support of the major donors.

The report was influential in encouraging a more positive stance by Germany, the United Kingdom, and Japan. It was a blueprint of potential value to the management, but there was still a low level of confidence by the donors in the capacity of the secretariat to undertake further reforms. Following a specially convened board meeting, they formed an Inter-Sessional Working Group to draw up a road-map for the organization. Developing countries were initially reluctant about further reforms, but seeing how narrow were the options they agreed to go along with the deliberations of the group. It produced a paper which became known—not entirely appropriately—as the "business plan." It was, in fact, much more broadly conceived: in effect a set of guidelines for future programs and organizational structure. For the only UN specialized agency to have been created mainly at the behest, and for the benefit, of the developing countries, the business plan amounted to an unprecedented degree of micro-management by a small minority of its richer members.

The business plan was formally adopted in June 1997. The plan required a clarification of scope, organization and funding. Scope was defined in terms of the twin goals of "strengthening of industrial capacities" and "cleaner and sustainable industrial development." The inclusion of energy was debated and excluded from the formal mandate on the grounds that it was a domain better covered by other more qualified organizations.[30] However, it soon found its way into UNIDO's activities.

At the end of 1997 a new director-general, Carlos A. Magariños, stepped into the breach with a clear mandate to implement a new phase of radical reform. He identified two types of problem: "emerging trends in the external environment affecting wider multilateral cooperation ... and aspects of UNIDO itself which gave rise to its relevance and the effectiveness of its performance."[31] The first type of problem became identified with the perception that UNIDO was more friendly to central planning at a time when a private sector-led, market-based paradigm had gained universal currency among donors. This view had its origins in the NIEO debate. It was consistently held by the influential right-wing US think-tank and inveterate UN critic, the Heritage Foundation, and had been repeated, for example, in the Danish Government's *Plan of Action for Active Multilateralism* (1996). The second problem area was internal and therefore more amenable to change.

Magariños came up with several principles for the transformation of UNIDO. He wanted a changing and adapting organization, embracing "wholesale" rather than "piecemeal" reform. He encouraged teamwork and cooperation across the organization, and the elimination of duplication. He made the business plan the blueprint for change and conceived the reform process in two stages: first, organizational (administrative, financial and structural); and second, programmatic.

Reorganization

Funding was still the root of the crisis, necessitating further cuts in staff and costs, such as travel. From 755 in 1997, staff numbers fell further to 630 over the next two years. As far as possible, the reductions were through natural wastage, with minimal involuntary redundancies.

Six divisions were reduced to three, as the business plan had advocated: a main substantive division, a division for technical cooperation and field services, and an administration and finance division. Each of these was to be headed by a managing director. The office of the director-general was also consolidated around fewer functions. These changes themselves represented a huge scaling down of management which had included five deputy directors-general (at the level of assistant UN secretary-general) as late as 1994 and now comprised just three managing directors in 1999 (at senior director level). The director-general, his chief of office and the managing directors formed the new executive board. At the second tier, there was also a board of directors bringing together the executive board with all directors of branches and regional bureaux. Retreats, workshops and team-building exercises were organized to help raise staff morale which had been adversely affected by more than five years of retrenchment.

The business plan had also advocated some decentralization to developing countries. There were several advantages. It would bring UNIDO closer to its clientele, permitting it to be more responsive in identifying and managing technical assistance programs, particularly as these programs were attempting to become more comprehensive at country level (see below). Field offices would also enhance visibility and enable the organization to align more closely to the rest of the UN system which was, in some cases (e.g. UNDP), already highly decentralized. (In 1997 the UN Secretary-General had also embarked on a reform program which stressed more UN coherence, particularly at the field level.)[32] With donors also moving to the field, there were advantages in fund mobilization.

UNIDO already had a limited field presence, but for a relatively small agency, the creation of numerous field offices presented problems of cost and coordination. UNIDO's solution was to establish a limited number of country offices, and create a network of regional offices to cover some of the rest. By the end of 1999 there were 23 full-fledged country offices and five regional offices headed by UNIDO representatives. An innovation which UNIDO pioneered in the 1970s led to a network of Investment and Technology Promotion Offices (ITPOs) designed to mobilize investors in developed countries to support project opportunities in developing and transition countries. The first "investment promotion service (IPS)" was set up in Brussels in 1975, and several ITPOs followed in the early 1980s. Italy also sponsored four Investment Promotion Units (IPUs) in North African countries, but these were wound up when funding stopped. Today, there are 11 ITPOs, all of them funded by the respective host governments (see Chapter 2).

Programming

A review of UNIDO's technical competences was also central to reform. If the organization was to find its place in an increasingly competitive development cooperation arena, it needed to decide what it was best at doing and what distinguished it from other sources of industrial services, including—and especially—those offered by the private sector. UNIDO was engaged in no fewer than 250 different types of activity. The aim was to designate a limited number of "services" and ensure that there was minimal overlap with other parts of the UN system and with outside organizations.

Origins and history of UNIDO 23

A "matrix" approach was encouraged, in order to allow countries to pick and mix services according to their specific needs. To be successful, the approach was dependent on a high degree of cross-organizational team-work. The tradition was otherwise. In 1997 there were no fewer than 1,700 separate projects in UNIDO, with an average size of $100,000. This scale of atomization was not unusual in a UN organization and it was symptomatic of a common problem. While size does not guarantee impact (small can also be catalytic), where there is a proliferation of small projects, there are also large numbers of project managers working mostly independently of each other. The result is incoherence and lack of sustainability.

As part of the reforms, therefore, UNIDO set out to consolidate its technical assistance around "integrated programs," comprising different combinations of services, which had been seen by the Danish assessment as one of the organization's comparative advantages. The first programs were conceived in 1998 and after two years, over 30 in all regions had begun implementation, with more in the pipeline. With improved programming practices came the need for better performance measurement, on which donors were insisting. Like other development agencies, UNIDO began measuring impact with more rigor and since 2002, in-depth evaluations have been undertaken for all the major integrated programs.[33]

From 2002, the process of consolidating services continued, but there was both semantics and substance in the compression of titles. Then in 2004, the introduction of "thematic areas" was considered. Using modernized language and resembling the overall strategic objectives of UNIDO, services were regrouped into clusters. The three themes were: poverty reduction through productive activities; trade capacity-building; and energy and environment. There was a fourth "cross-cutting" area, assistance to countries emerging from crisis.

The "trade" and "crisis" priorities signified that UNIDO was moving into two new areas of opportunity. Trade capacity-building was recognition of the growing importance of export opportunities for developing country enterprises, but also the need to meet the scale and standards required by global markets and by linkages to international value-chains.

The crisis theme was a response to the growing involvement of the UN system in major reconstruction programs in fragile states. From 2004, several major UN trust funds were established to support the work of the agencies and UNIDO has developed and implemented post-conflict programs in Afghanistan, Indonesia, Iraq, Sudan and Uganda (see Box 1.2). These programs helped both to restore and create enterprises to support the livelihoods of formerly war-torn communities. In Laos, there was a different context of recovery. Working with the UN Office on Drugs and Crime (UNODC), UNIDO has helped to create income opportunities that are an alternative to opium poppy cultivation for hundreds of villagers recovering from addiction to illicit drugs.

Given the central importance of the industrialization process to development, UNIDO can also be considered well-placed to contribute to conflict prevention:

> Whereas in the past the role of development agencies in social conflict has been limited to the processes of post-conflict reconstruction, the inseparable natures of environmental, employment-related, and economic concerns today, require a preventive lens in shaping the social environment. UNIDO's triple mandate assigns the organization an important role in this context, and possibly a comparative advantage over other organizations.[34]

By 2008, UNIDO had 40 projects in 17 post-conflict countries with a total value of $40 million. Evaluations of a sample of these projects have reported mixed impacts. UNIDO has not sought to make more of this role in fragile states, and there is no corporate strategy on post-crisis projects.[35] The cross-cutting theme was later mainstreamed as an area of activity under the poverty reduction objective.

Box 1.2 UNIDO in Iraq

With funding support from the UN's Iraq Trust Fund, UNIDO implemented two major programs in the country between 2004 and 2007. In the Thi-qar Governorate of southern Iraq, UNIDO teamed with the UN Food and Agriculture Organization (FAO) to help 1,500 households establish small-scale enterprises. Three training centers were established to provide technical, managerial and marketing skills using local instructors. Many new viable enterprises resulted in various sectors including food processing, metal-working, wood-working and textiles.

In the second program, UNIDO helped to rehabilitate a major dairy plant in the center of the country. Through technical assistance and provision of new technology milk output was restored and made safe for the consumption of 100,000 Iraqis, mainly children. The program was a pilot, designed to be emulated throughout the country's dairy sector, demonstrating good practice in management, processing, marketing and distribution.

At the beginning of 2006, Kandeh Yumkella became director-general. Having joined UNIDO 10 years earlier, spending time both at headquarters and in the field (Nigeria), and becoming a special advisor to Magariños in 2003, Yumkella had lived through and helped implement the post-1997 reforms. He saw his task as building on the changes he had witnessed, or as he called it: "consolidating and deepening the reform process."[36] As an insider, he has been successful in raising staff morale in the organization. He has increased management transparency and enhanced internal communications. He has expanded staff training substantially and encouraged mobility within UNIDO, both horizontally between headquarters and field, and vertically through internal promotions. With 25 percent of the staff retiring between 2009 and 2013 (coinciding with his second four-year term of office), the DG has also been provided with an unprecedented opportunity for renewal which has been pursued through an external merit-based recruitment drive. Between 2006 and 2009 nearly 200 new staff were recruited, some of them through a newly instituted *Young Professionals Program.*

With the encouragement (and funding) of donors, UNIDO has instituted results-based management, applying performance criteria to staff as well as programs. A new Bureau for Organizational Strategy and Learning was established to oversee program quality.

Broad continuity has been maintained in UNIDO's programming priorities. The three themes of poverty reduction through productive activities, trade capacity building, and energy and environment have been reaffirmed. The first priority has accorded more emphasis to private-sector development, particularly among small enterprises in poorer communities. Trade capacity-building has expanded in scope as UNIDO has overtaken UNCTAD and the International Trade Centre (ITC) as the UN development system's largest trade-related TA organization in terms of spending. Energy and environment are a mix of old (work on the Montreal Protocol) and new, with renewable energy and climate change gaining prominence. In the UN development system, energy has always been something of an orphan—which may explain why it received relatively little attention in the Millennium Declaration of 2000 which helped to establish the system's development agenda up to 2015. In order to give a boost to the UN's work in this area, the UN development system's Chief Executives' Board (CEB) established a coordinating mechanism of 18 interested agencies (plus the World Bank) which it designated UN-Energy. In 2007 the UNIDO director-general was appointed as its chair. The UN Secretary-General also established a High-Level Group on Sustainable Energy in 2011 and asked the UNIDO director-general to co-chair it (see milestones, Box 1.4).

Conclusion

UNIDO's history has been marked by advances and setbacks, as well as far-reaching changes in its structure and orientation. What it has revealed are disagreements among its principal donor sponsors about the proper role of an international public organization devoted to the industrialization process, but also a strong and unwavering fealty to its objectives by developing countries.

Partly because of donor doubts, funding (discussed in more detail in Chapter 2) has been a preoccupation from the very beginning and it remains so. UNIDO's core resources have remained stable (but will be threatened if the United Kingdom, which contributes about 9 percent, carries out its threat to withdraw at the end of 2012; see Box 1.3). Continuing growth—and even sustaining its current levels of activity—will depend on raising additional TA resources. The dilemma for UNIDO is to know how to take advantage of new funding opportunities, while not allowing itself to be pulled in too many directions which muddy its mandate and strain its technical capacities. Within the three thematic priorities, there are now over 20 separate areas of responsibility. Some of these are dependent on the earmarked sponsorship of individual donors, and therefore more in the nature of bilateral assistance under a multilateral umbrella ("multi-bi").

Funding patterns are nevertheless indicative of development trends, which point to opportunities for UNIDO. In 2010 environment and energy programs accounted for 44 percent of UNIDO's total TA spending, against 31 percent for the poverty priority and 23 percent for trade capacity-building.[37] UNIDO's efforts in "greening industry" and enhancing access to renewable energy can play to its strengths and can attract growing support (see Chapter 6). Also in the trade area, UNIDO has successfully taken advantage of growing funding opportunities and now has the largest trade-related TA program in the UN system, ahead of the two "trade agencies," UNCTAD and the ITC (see Chapter 5).

> **Box 1.3 The United Kingdom and UNIDO**
>
> In 2004–05 the Department for International Development (DfID) of the United Kingdom undertook an assessment of UNIDO as part of a review of the effectiveness of the 23 multilateral institutions with which DfID has an institutional partnership. The Multilateral Effectiveness Framework (MEFF) provided an independent confirmation of the wisdom of the reforms undertaken by UNIDO and the initiatives introduced after 1997. The MEFF confirmed that reform had increased the cost-effectiveness and

relevance of UNIDO and helped to increase technical cooperation delivery. It praised the commitment to the Millennium Development Goals and to the partnerships with UN and other organizations. The MEFF rated UNIDO as "the best organization among the UN standard-setting agencies."[38]

In 2010–11 DfID undertook another Multilateral Aid Review of 43 development agencies, including UNIDO. In "value for money terms" it was rated "poor". It had made "good progress in its cost consciousness and demonstrated good partnership behavior," but it was "not aligned with UK aid priorities and does not play a critical role in delivering the Millennium Development Goals (MDGs)...It has unsatisfactory results reporting and financial management."[39] In a complete reversal of its position a few years earlier, in 2011 the United Kingdom announced its withdrawal from UNIDO (to take effect from the end of 2012).

Organizationally, UNIDO is now on a sounder footing under committed leadership. The next chapter provides more details of its present structure and further anticipated reforms. Its long-term survival, however, will depend more than ever on its ability to demonstrate the kind of results that are unique to its mandate and technical capacities.

Box 1.4 UNIDO milestones

1954	First full UN study of industrialization
1956	Establishment of Industry Section in UN; first program of work on industrialization
1959	UN Industry Section upgraded to Branch
1961	General Assembly resolution 1712 establishes UN Centre for Industrial Development
1965	GA resolution 20/89 establishes UNIDO as special organization of the UN
1967	UNIDO formally established in Vienna
1975	Second General Conference: Lima Declaration includes recommendation to convert UNIDO to UN specialized agency
1979	UNIDO Constitution drawn up
1986	UNIDO becomes UN specialized agency. Mr Domingo L. Siazon becomes first Director-General
1993	Fifth General Conference (Yaoundé) recommends reforms. Mr Mauricio de Maria y Campos becomes second Director-General

1994   Withdrawal of Canada
1995   Commission on Global Governance recommends closure of UNIDO. Withdrawal of United States
1997   Danish assessment of UNIDO. Withdrawal of Australia. Business Plan approved. Mr Carlos Magariños becomes third Director-General (December)
2005   Member states approve the Strategic Long-term Vision Statement
2006   Mr Kandeh Yumkella becomes fourth Director-General
2007   UNIDO asked to coordinate UN's work on energy
2011   UNIDO director-general designated as co-chair of the High-Level Group on Sustainable Energy

Box 1.5 UNIDO heads

1967–74: Ibrahim Helmi Abdel-Rahman (Egypt), Executive Director

With degrees from the universities of Cairo and Cambridge, he was a university science lecturer until 1954, when he quit academia to become Cabinet secretary. In 1960 he established the Institute of National Planning in Cairo and was responsible for drafting the first five-year development plan for Egypt, 1960–65. He joined the UN secretariat in 1963 as Commissioner, heading the Centre for Industrial Development, becoming the first head of UNIDO when it was established within the UN in 1967.

1975–85: Abd-El Rahman Khane (Algeria), Executive Director

Trained as a physician, he became the head of l'Organisme Saharien, responsible for overseeing the exploitation of the country's oil resources, when Algeria became independent in 1962, a post he held for 10 years. From 1966 to 1970 he was concurrently Minister of Public Works and Construction. In 1972 he was appointed head of the general secretariat of OPEC, also based in Vienna, becoming executive director of UNIDO in January 1975.

1986–93: Domingo L. Siazon (Philippines), Director-General

With degrees from the universities of Ateneo de Manila, Tokyo and Harvard, he first followed a diplomatic career from 1964 with appointments in Japan and Switzerland. In 1973 he helped establish the Philippine Embassy in Vienna, becoming resident representative to the IAEA. From 1977 he was the permanent representative to UNIDO and in 1980 also became the Ambassador of the Philippines to Austria.

1993–96: Mauricio de Maria y Campos (Mexico), Director-General

Educated at the National University of Mexico and at Sussex (United Kingdom), he joined the government where he served in various capacities. In 1974 he was Director-General for foreign investment at the Ministry of Trade and Industry, later moving to the Ministry of Finance. In 1982 he was appointed vice-minister for industrial development and from 1989 executive vice-president of Banco Mexicano (SOMEX), responsible for strategic planning. He joined UNIDO in 1992 as Deputy Director-General before moving to the top job a year later.

1997–2005: Carlos A. Magariños (Argentina), Director-General

Graduating with an MBA from the University of Buenos Aires, he worked as a consultant before becoming national director for foreign trade and then Under-Secretary of State for Industry in 1992 and Secretary of State for Industry and Mining the following year. In 1996 he was appointed as economic and trade representative in Washington, DC, with the rank of Ambassador, taking over at UNIDO in December 1997 at the age of 36.

2005–present: Kandeh Yumkella (Sierra Leone), Director-General

With degrees from the universities of Njala (Sierra Leone), Cornell and Illinois, he commenced an academic career in the United States before returning to Sierra Leone in 1994, where he was appointed Minister for Trade, Industry and State Enterprises. In 1995 he joined UNIDO where he served in various capacities, including special advisor to the UNIDO Director-General, Director for Africa as well as Director of the first UNIDO regional office in Nigeria.

2 Current structure and mandate

- Mission statement
- Revised structure
- Programming and evaluation
- UNIDO's field presence
- Investment and Technology Promotion Offices
- Governance
- Partnerships
- South-South cooperation
- Resource mobilization
- Conclusion

This chapter provides an anatomy of UNIDO as it is today. As the previous chapter made clear, the last two decades have seen substantial upheavals in the organization, for reasons partly within its control, and partly not. Building on the strengths regained by the organization in the past decade, the present director-general has accelerated the pace of reform since assuming office in December 2005.

From 2011, UNIDO has had a new mission statement and has reorganized the secretariat further, resulting in more consolidation. Maintaining a field presence presents a challenge for a modest-sized organization, but it has co-located some of its country representatives with the UN Development Programme (UNDP) and a set of regional offices each covering several countries. There are also Investment and Technology Promotion Offices (ITPOs) in both developed and developing countries, but they are not closely integrated with the rest of the organization.

Partnerships have become important to the organization in its contemporary phase. As described in the last chapter, within the UN development system UNIDO was originally charged with "coordinating industrial development activities." In a continuum from agricultural production, through agro-industry and processing, to exports, UNIDO finds itself working alongside other parts of the system such as the Food and Agriculture Organization of the UN (FAO), the UN Conference on Trade and Development (UNCTAD) and the International Trade Centre (ITC), necessitating cooperation with these and other organizations. In recent years UNIDO has taken on a growing role in the area of energy, strengthening its partnership with the UN Environment Programme (UNEP). This chapter will also look at UNIDO's relationships with other international public and private organizations working in similar fields, and its commitment to help foster more South-South cooperation.

Finally, the chapter looks at the resource situation and the evolution of funding since the very difficult decade of the 1990s.

Mission statement

In 2011 UNIDO continued its reform, based on a Programme for Change and Organizational Renewal (PCOR), which is expected to be completed at the end of 2013, co-terminous with the contract of the present director-general. UNIDO's activities were still to be grouped under the three broad priority headings of poverty reduction through productive activities; trade capacity-building; and energy and environment; however, it launched a new mission statement, the content of which reflects a more go-ahead and business-like image. In a more dynamic vein, UNIDO offers prosperity and partnership through "growth with quality," emphasizing environmental sustainability and results, and seeking a more holistic approach by "delivering as one UNIDO." It reads like the summary of a new business plan (see Box 2.1) and it is also linked to eight goals (four strategic, four operational) which UNIDO aims to achieve in 2012.

Box 2.1 UNIDO mission statement

Partner for prosperity

UNIDO aspires to reduce poverty through sustainable industrial development. We want every country to have the opportunity to grow a flourishing productive sector, to increase their participation in international trade and to safeguard their environment.

> ***Our services: growth with quality***
>
> Growth with quality means that we continuously improve and grow all our services, which are multidisciplinary and positively transform policies and institutions worldwide.
>
> We offer solutions: Bring global expertise and experience to address complex development challenges through integrated and high-impact services.
>
> We are flexible: Differentiate and adapt our approaches and methodologies according to the needs of countries at different stages of development.
>
> We expand our services: Widen our geographic scope and increase our delivery volume to serve more countries and people.
>
> We ensure effectiveness: Measure the impact that our services have on development in order to ensure the best possible results.
>
> ***Our operations: delivering as one UNIDO***
>
> Delivering as one UNIDO means that we are united in purpose and actions.
>
> We empower our people: Recognize and develop competencies and knowledge, encourage communication and innovative thinking, strengthen integrity and accountability and reward team achievement.
>
> We serve our stakeholders: Advance a culture of cooperation, responsiveness and ownership in addressing the needs of all our stakeholders.
>
> We lead by example: Demonstrate ethical and gender-sensitive leadership, motivate people, promote innovation and work in flexible and cross-organizational teams.
>
> We manage efficiently: Improve the timeliness and cost-efficiency of all our services and create and use business processes that minimize bureaucracy.

Revised structure

As part of the ongoing reform process, the structure of the secretariat has also been frequently adjusted. The most recent restructuring took place in 2011, resulting in some further consolidation. The main technical division now comprises six technical branches (and a results-monitoring unit). Two of these—Agri-business Development and Business, Investment and Technology Services—encompassed activities under the first "poverty reduction" priority. Trade Capacity Building contributed to the priority with the same title, while there were three branches—Energy and Climate Change, Environmental Management and Montreal Protocol—responsible for the third priority of energy and environment (see Figure 2.1). The correspondence between branches and priorities, however, is not an exact one given the broad cross-cutting expression of priorities.

The technical division also absorbed the field operations, including the five regional offices. These had previously been part of the "strategies" division and the intention was to bring substantive and geographical staff into closer alignment, strengthening the programming

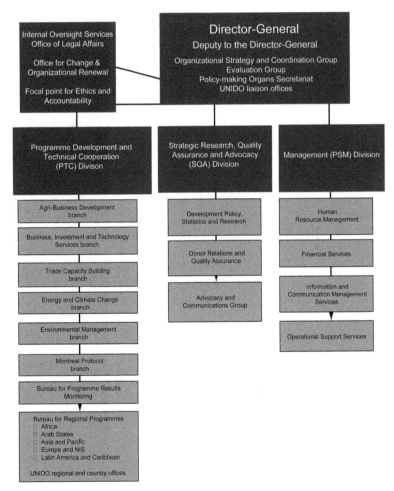

Figure 2.1 UNIDO organizational structure

responsibilities of the latter. This gradual consolidation of the organization over the years has occurred in tandem with stability in numbers of staff and an increase in technical assistance (TA) resources. In the late 1990s the regular (core) and extra-budgetary (non-core) resources were at broadly similar levels, while in 2010 the ratio was almost 1:2 (see Table 2.2).

The second division, now shorn of field operations, concentrates on development policy and research, while administrative and financial management is in a third division. The offices of the director-general and his deputy[1] contain several units concerned with organizational strategy and reform as well as auditing and evaluation.

UNIDO counted just over 700 staff in total at the end of 2010, 300 in the professional category (including 36 national professional officers in the field) and 400 support staff. Nearly 80 percent of staff were in the Vienna headquarters, the rest in country and regional offices in developing countries, as well as in the 11 ITPOs, and the three liaison offices (see below). Among professional staff, there is quite a strong male bias (71 percent), which is particularly marked at the managerial levels. A Gender Mainstreaming Steering Committee was established in 2009 to begin redressing the imbalance and eventually achieve parity in the secretariat.

Programming and evaluation

As part of the ongoing internal PCOR reforms, the process of developing and approving programs has recently been revamped in order to raise their quality. *Ex ante*, the initial scrutiny of project requests is first undertaken by a screening and technical review committee in the main technical division. Since the objective is to separate screening and approval, these requests are then forwarded to an appraisal group in the other division and then examined in a third stage by a cross-organizational Programme Approval and Monitoring Committee (AMC). In 2010 the approval rate of submissions to the AMC (then known as the Program Approval Committee) was 70 percent. The change in name of the approval committee is also significant, since it is mandated to undertake monitoring functions which will review the composition of UNIDO's project portfolio by regional and thematic priority, as well as funding sources. A new Programme Results Monitoring Unit has also been created in the Programme Development and Technical Cooperation (PTC) Division.

The need for more monitoring of projects was recommended by a peer review of UNIDO's evaluation functions undertaken in 2010.[2] The report was generally positive about UNIDO's efforts to strengthen the role of the Evaluation Group (EVA), recommending that the "evaluatability" of programs should be enhanced further to determine impact and outcomes. UNIDO revised its evaluation policy in 2006 and has instituted a results-based management system.

The challenge for UNIDO—as with many other UN organizations—has been the need to make a sustainable impact with limited resources spread over many industry-related disciplines and many countries. In 2010 304 new projects were approved, to add to 2,175 ongoing in a total of 100 countries and regions. It was to respond to such dispersal that UNIDO instituted integrated country programs in the late 1990s. Some 30 of these have been implemented and in 2010 EVA undertook a review of the evaluations of 11 of those launched between 2002 and 2005.[3] The review found mixed results. Apart from the familiar variations in program management performance, success was generally correlated with the degree of commitment of the beneficiary country. Results were variable and impact was often limited by insufficient resources.[4]

UNIDO's field presence

UNIDO is a well-dispersed organization, in consideration of its overall size. It has a presence in 49 developing country capitals, several offices covering more than one country. Nineteen of these representatives are in sub-Saharan Africa. In addition, it has ITPOs in developing and industrialized countries, designed to encourage investment in developing countries. There are also three liaison offices which maintain contact with other UN agencies and permanent missions (Geneva and New York) and the European Commission (Brussels) (see Table 2.1).

UNIDO has maintained a strong tradition of outreach. From its days as a department of the UN secretariat, UNIDO fielded a network of senior industrial development field advisers (SIDFAs) who were generally co-located with the UNDP resident representatives (along with similar advisors from FAO).[5] After becoming a specialized agency, UNIDO began opening its own offices, headed by full-fledged representatives, but many of these were wound down during the crisis of the mid-1990s. Most of the field offices have been re-opened during the last 15 years. The SIDFA model was revisited more recently when in 2004 an agreement was reached with UNDP to host "UNIDO desks" in a selection of its country offices. The aims were to strengthen UNIDO representation in the countries concerned, as well as to develop joint programs on

Table 2.1 UNIDO offices and representations outside Vienna

	SSA	Asia-Pacific	West Asia-North Africa	Americas	Eastern Europe & Turkey	Western Europe
Field offices	Burkina Faso Cameroon Côte d'Ivoire DR Congo Eritrea Ethiopia (R) Ghana Guinea Kenya Madagascar Mali Mozambique Nigeria Rwanda Senegal Sierra Leone South Africa (R) Sudan Uganda Tanzania Zimbabwe (21)	Bangladesh China (R) Cambodia India (R) Indonesia Laos Pakistan Philippines Thailand Vietnam (10)	Afghanistan Algeria Egypt (R) Iran Jordan Lebanon (R) Morocco Tunisia (8)	Bolivia Brazil Colombia Ecuador Mexico Nicaragua Uruguay (R) (7)	Armenia Kyrgyzstan Turkey (3)	

Table 2.1 (continued)

SSA	Asia-Pacific	West Asia-North Africa	Americas	Eastern Europe & Turkey	Western Europe
Investment & Technology Promotion Offices	Japan (Tokyo) China (Shanghai and Beijing) South Korea (Seoul) (4)	Bahrain (1)	Mexico (Mexico City) (1)	Russia (Moscow) (1)	Belgium (Brussels) France (Marseille) United Kingdom (Warrington) Italy (Rome) (4)
Liaison Offices			USA (New York)		Switzerland (Geneva) Belgium (Brussels)

private-sector development. The present director-general has increased the exchange of staff between headquarters and the field.

Investment and Technology Promotion Offices (ITPOs)

UNIDO's mandate has always included the promotion of investment and technology transfer as a means of stimulating industrial development. The first "investment promotion service" was set up in 1975 in Brussels and more offices followed in the 1980s in several European countries. The purpose of the ITPOs, as they became known, was to identify and mobilize outward investors in the developed host countries with an interest in industrial projects in developing countries (see Box 2.2). The ITPOs organized investment forums for the purpose and promoted matchmaking between potential partners. Some of the European ITPOs have since closed, but others have opened in Bahrain and China, with an orientation more toward capacity-building of national investment promotion agencies.

An evaluation in 2010[6] found that the ITPOs had made a modest contribution to industrial development in some countries. Their full potential was not being realized, however, and they should be more fully integrated with the developmental mandate and the technical assistance activities of UNIDO. If more ITPOs were opened in developing countries, there would be an opportunity to create full-fledged national UNIDO centers acting as versatile outposts of the organization and offering a full range of industrial promotion services.

Box 2.2 **Four objectives of ITPOs**

- Disseminate the latest information on legal and economic conditions, investment financing and opportunities for industrial cooperation;
- Identify and promote specific investment opportunities;
- Provide expert advice at all stages of the business cycle; and
- Facilitate business contacts between project sponsors and potential foreign investors.

Governance

UNIDO's principal governing body is the General Conference, which is now convened every two years and attended by the full membership. There are currently 174 member states, the most recent adherents being

Montenegro (2006), Samoa (2008), and Tuvalu (2011). The conference formally approves the biennial work program and budget and appoints the directors-general for four-year terms. The General Conference appoints the Industrial Development Board which comprises 53 member states: 33 from developing countries, five from Eastern Europe, and 15 from developed countries. It is the main oversight body and meets annually. The board oversees the work of the organization and makes recommendations to the conference on policy matters. It has a subsidiary organ, the Program and Budget Committee, comprising 27 member states, which meets once a year. The committee assists the board in preparing and examining the budget and the work program and advising on other financial matters.

Individual General Conferences have been key markers in UNIDO's history. The first "special international conference" on UNIDO was held in Vienna in 1971 at the organization's new home. Four years later, the second conference was held in Lima, Peru and resulted in the declaration to convert UNIDO to a specialized agency of the UN. After conferences in Vienna and New Delhi, the fifth conference was not held until 1993 in Yaoundé, Cameroon, but was important because it approved the first of several major reform programs. From 1993, the conferences became biennial and have all subsequently been held in Vienna (largely for budgetary reasons). The conference of 1997 was again significant for its approval of another major reform program during a continuing phase of crisis.

Partnerships

The current management has been assiduous in developing UNIDO's working relationships with other partners. This starts with the UN family itself. In 2006 UNIDO was an active partner in the reform program of the UN Secretary-General, who had established a High-Level Panel on System-wide Coherence, chaired by three serving prime ministers.[7] The report resulted in a recommendation, among others, for a more unified UN-wide approach to programming and delivery at the country level—the so-called One UN initiative, which commenced in eight pilot countries. UNIDO's engagement in joint programs has been facilitated by having field representation in nearly 50 countries. A joint agreement with UNDP led to the establishment of UNIDO desks in 16 UNDP country offices around the world. The director-general was asked by the UN Secretary-General in 2007 to become the chair of UN-Energy, a loose consortium of concerned UN entities, which aims to foster closer collaboration in energy-related activities. In 2011 he became co-chair (with the Bank of America chairman) of the High-Level Group on Sustainable Energy for All, which will campaign for universal access to modern energy services by 2030.

A partnership with FAO focuses on the need to meet mounting global challenges related to agri-business and agro-industry development and bio-energy. In addition to joint projects, it has resulted in a number of technical manuals and toolkits. With the International Fund for Agricultural Development (IFAD), UNIDO has collaborated in helping countries with the development of value chains and market linkages for agro-industry, agro-processing, food production and bio-energy.

Cooperation with the International Labour Organization (ILO) focuses on issues concerning youth and women, two particularly vulnerable groups in developing countries. Both organizations are partners, for example, in a regional program among the Mano River Union countries (Côte d'Ivoire, Guinea, Liberia and Sierra Leone), which addresses the dangerous links between youth unemployment and insecurity. Elsewhere in Africa, ILO and UNIDO have jointly formulated entrepreneurship development training programs designed to strengthen capacities in private-sector agencies and non-governmental organizations (NGOs), and to support businesswomen and young entrepreneurs in the establishment of competitive micro- and small-scale agri-businesses.

UNIDO has forged partnerships with other UN organizations in the area of trade. With the World Trade Organization (WTO), UNCTAD, ITC, UNDP and the five UN regional commissions, it is part of a UN cluster on trade and productive capacity. The cluster advocates for the inclusion of trade in national poverty-reduction strategies and in UN country programming frameworks (UNDAFs). With WTO, UNIDO also has joint activities on trade capacity-building and on enhancing manufacturing and export capacities in selected industrial sectors of developing countries. UNIDO is an implementing agency in the Enhanced Integrated Framework (EIF) in WTO's Aid for Trade initiative and actively contributes to the WTO-led Standards and Trade Development Facility (STDF) on Sanitary and Phyto-Sanitary (SPS) issues (see Chapter 6).

The relationship with the UNEP has been especially close as UNIDO has expanded its activities in energy and environment. The collaboration is marked by a joint program to establish National Cleaner Production Centers in 42 countries, aimed at reducing pollutants, improving efficiency and enhancing the productivity of industrial processes, in part through the introduction of new technologies. With UNEP and UNDP, UNIDO is an implementing partner of the Montreal Protocol and the Global Environment Facility (GEF) for projects related to ozone depletion, persistent organic pollutants and climate change (see Chapter 6).

UNIDO also has links with several major global corporations. In the area of information technology (IT), it has established a partnership with Hewlett-Packard focused on training in IT and other skills to equip unemployed youth in Africa and in the Arab region to set up and run their own small businesses. A joint UNIDO/Microsoft partnership also aims to enhance both the transfer of skills and the competitiveness of small and medium-sized enterprises (SMEs). A refurbishment program launched in Uganda will provide affordable computers to SMEs and similar programs are planned elsewhere in Africa, as well as in the Caribbean. Entrepreneurship training is also the focus of a secondary school program supported by Chevron in Angola. A more broad-based program has been established with the support of Ecobank Transnational Incorporated, a pan-African banking group. The partnership will support agri-business and agro-industrial activities, with emphasis on energy sustainability.

UNIDO has also been strengthening its links with academia and maintains many university partnerships. In 2006, with three European universities in Austria, Italy and the Netherlands, it established the University Chair on Innovation (UNCHAIN). This initiative has led to the establishment of a network of similar university chairs, twinning universities in developing countries around the Mediterranean (Egypt, Lebanon, Morocco, Syria, and Tunisia) with the original three. The development of bio-technologies for industrial development is the focus of a partnership with the University of Ghent, Belgium, which has led to the establishment of a network of public research institutions in developing and developed countries. UNIDO has ties with two of the institutes of the United Nations University. With the Maastricht Economic Research Institute of Innovation and Technology (MERIT) in the Netherlands, UNIDO participates in research and training on science and technology innovation. With the World Institute for Development Economics Research (WIDER) in Finland and MERIT, UNIDO is collaborating on research into the nature of industrialization processes.

In 2011 UNIDO combined with the Said Business School of the University of Oxford to establish the Institute for Capacity Development. The institute is designed to foster dialogue, share experience and provide training on issues pertaining to sustainable industrial development. As part of UNIDO's global forum role, it aspires to become a "virtual resource center" for an international community of practice on industrial development. The first course, held near Vienna with a faculty of academics and UNIDO staff, brought together 35 senior officials from 30 countries to discuss global strategies and negotiating skills around the subject of green growth.

South-South cooperation

UNIDO's sponsorship of the ITPOs, mentioned above, is an example of its efforts to promote South-South cooperation, by encouraging more horizontal investment flows. In recent years UNIDO has added its name and its funding to other institutions to foster cooperation among developing countries. In 2007 the UNIDO Centre for South-South Industrial Cooperation (UCSSIC) was opened in New Delhi. India does not have an ITPO, and one role of the center will be to promote outward investment and technology partnerships. Drawing on expertise available within India, it will also encourage exchange in areas such as renewable energy (wind and biomass); low-cost housing and building materials; food processing and agro-industries; pharmaceuticals, aromatics, traditional remedies and biotechnology; automobile components and machine-tools; and IT. The UCSSIC is also a partner in a training facility established in 2010 in Hyderabad, India, designed to strengthen the skills of the staff and management of quality testing laboratories in developing countries (see Chapter 5). Also in India, UNIDO has established a Regional Centre for Small Hydro-Power in Trivandrum, one of three such centers in the developing world. There is a second Regional Centre for Small Hydro-Power in Abuja, Nigeria, to serve the West Africa region, and in China UNIDO has co-sponsored the International Centre for Small Hydro-Power in Hangzhou, which has a global remit. Also in the energy field, UNIDO has collaborated with the Turkish Government in setting up, in 2004, the International Centre for Hydrogen Energy Technologies (ICHET) in Istanbul. (These centers are discussed in Chapter 6.)

Resource mobilization

As discussed in the previous chapter, UNIDO's funding history has been akin to a roller-coaster ride. As the alpine profile of Figure 2.2 reveals, contributions dipped in the 1980s and plunged after 1990, heralding a full decade of resource decline. The bottom of the valley was only reached as the century turned. By 2010, the total expenditures of UNIDO were still below the level of 1990 but, as the management is keen to stress, the organization is now doing more with fewer staff, signifying a productivity gain.

The last few years have been successful in terms of resource mobilization, with non-core TA expenditures increasing from US$113 million in 2005 to $154 million in 2010, yielding average annual growth of nearly 7 percent (see Figure 2.2 and Table 2.2). UNIDO received over

Current structure and mandate 43

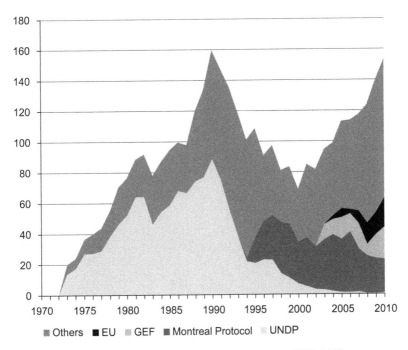

Figure 2.2 UNIDO extra-budgetary spending by source, 1972–2010

$80 million from bilateral donors (within "Industrial Development Fund and other trust funds," Table 2.2). The most important bilateral sources in 2010 were, in descending order: Italy ($16.5 million), Japan ($5.2 million), Switzerland ($4.8 million), Norway ($4.4 million), Russia ($3.8 million), Germany ($2.9 million), France ($2.7 million), Canada ($2.2 million), and Austria ($2.0 million).[8] These nine donors thus accounted for over half the bilateral sources. However, encouragingly, UNIDO also received several important contributions from developing countries: almost $2 million from Nigeria and over $1 million each from India and Zambia. The so-called "self-financed trust funds" contributed by developing countries were worth over $3.7 million. Thus, in spite of continuing dependence on a few of its traditional bilateral donors, UNIDO's sources have become more diversified.

In recent years UNIDO has also secured substantial funding from the world's largest TA grant donor, the European Commission, which is a solid supporter of the quality conformity programs which facilitate entry into European markets. Having a liaison office in Brussels has helped to develop and expand this relationship.

Table 2.2 UNIDO expenditures by source, 1970–2010 (current US$ million)

	1970	1975	1980	1985	1990	1995	2000	2005	2010
Regular budget resources	11.7	21.9	50.5	52.6	100.4	130.6	61.2	98.3	108.7
Regular budget	10.2	19.9	47.0	49.3	95.9	121.2	59.8	93.1	104.4
Regular budget technical assistance	1.5	2.0	3.5	3.3	4.5	9.4	1.4	5.2	4.3
Extrabudgetary resources	20.2	36.5	76.3	94.5	155.1	108.5	67.2	107.7	149.2
UNDP	8.2	27.0	52.0	58.7	88.7	20.6	7.0	1.2	0.8
Montreal Protocol	-	-	-	-	-	16.6	27.1	34.8	22.0
Global Environment Facility	-	-	-	-	-	-	-	14.1	20.9
European Commission	-	-	-	-	-	-	-	5.8	19.0
Industrial Development Fund and other trust funds	12.0	9.5	24.3	35.8	70.9	71.3	33.1	51.8	86.5
Total	31.9	58.4	126.8	147.1	255.5	239.7	128.4	206.0	257.9

Source: *Yearbook of the United Nations* (New York: various years); *UNIDO Annual Reports* (Vienna: various years)

UNIDO has also become a recipient of several other multilateral funding sources. As already mentioned, UNIDO is a beneficiary of the Global Environment Facility and the Multilateral Fund of the Montreal Protocol which accounted for 29 percent of the total extrabudgetary resource spending in 2010. It has also become an "implementing partner" of the *Enhanced Integrated Framework*, an aid-for-trade fund managed by the WTO for the benefit of Least Developed Countries. UNIDO has successfully tapped into the various "multi-partner" trust funds that have been established for individual countries, as well as the Spanish-funded Millennium Development Goals (MDG) Achievement Fund which benefits 49 countries. Since 2004, a total of $4.5 billion has been paid into these funds, mainly by the traditional donor governments, and about $3.2 billion has been spent. These funds are channeled through about 40 UN entities (including subsidiaries). By the end of 2010, UNIDO had expended over $65 million from these sources, the largest share coming from the Iraq Recovery Fund (see Table 2.3).

Table 2.3 UNIDO expenditures from UN multi-partner trust funds, 2004–10 (US$ million)

Fund	Total expenditures	UNIDO expenditures
Iraq Trust Fund	1,193.1	41.0
MDG Achievement Fund	243.5	8.9
Lebanon Recovery Fund	28.5	4.3
"One UN" Country Funds	282.4	10.5
All other funds		1.0
Total	3,170.0	65.7

Source: mdtf.undp.org/portfolio/fund

Conclusion

The restoration of UNIDO's funding levels in the past decade has allowed it to build back while consolidating the secretariat structure and strengthening its internal systems of quality control. As for other UN organizations, however, the resources situation remains vulnerable. Partly this is due to renewed resource constraints among the traditional donors (although the imminent withdrawal of the United Kingdom has occurred in spite of that country's commitment to continue increasing its aid budget). Vulnerability is also related to a greater reliance on non-core funding which is always more volatile than core contributions. On the positive side, the diversification of sources to include more developing and transition-economy countries is a doubly positive sign, since it spreads the risks of volatility, as well as solidifying important client-provider relationships.

The development of new connections and partnerships, not only within the UN family and with emerging economy governments, but more especially with the international private sector will, in UNIDO's words, "increase the impact of its technical cooperation as well as promote major issues related to industrial development."[9] Some of these partnerships are lucrative for the organization and its program countries and they help to raise awareness of the importance of industrialization. All of them also assist in raising UNIDO's visibility. Some will undoubtedly prove to be more enduring than others and, given the size of the organization, UNIDO will in the future need to confine its attention to those from which it can leverage the most advantage.

3 Research and policy

- Statistics
- Research
- Industrial competitiveness
- Industrial policy
- Evolving models
- Policy principles
- Policies in practice
- Conclusion

The Introduction highlighted two fundamental considerations which underlie the *raison d'être* of UNIDO: the importance of industrialization to development, and the role of industrial policy. The long tradition of research and analysis in UNIDO, from its days as a division in the UN secretariat when it specialized in industrial studies, reflects the importance for the organization of addressing these concerns: respectively, providing empirical evidence of the industrialization record in developing countries, and making the case for industrial policy. This chapter describes UNIDO's activities in these two areas.

Both tasks—research and policy—are important for the second of UNIDO's basic functions, as presaged by its constitution (see Box 1.1 in Chapter 1), namely "global forum facilitator" (the other being technical assistance). UNIDO was an important conduit in the 1970s for the demands of the developing countries for a fairer global economic balance under the new international development order (see Chapter 1), and it has retained a role as a forum for debate on the role of industrialization. UNIDO's research and policy outputs serve as basic documentation for these forums, as well as helping to animate the broader global deliberations on development. UNIDO describes this role as allowing "for various actors in the public and private sectors, civil society organizations and the policymaking community to establish dialogue and develop partnerships," involving the generation and dissemination of "knowledge relating to industrial development."[1]

This chapter reviews UNIDO's activities in statistics and research, including the publication of its main flagship, the *Industrial Development Report*. It goes on to describe its tool to measure industrial competitiveness, as a basis for countries to measure their performance and shape their policies. Finally, there is a description of UNIDO's work in industrial policy, which forms the basis of its own advocacy in this area.

There is a long tradition of research in UNIDO from its days as a division in the UN secretariat in the 1950s and 1960s, when it specialized in industrial studies. Over the years, it has retained this capacity and has been the source of some original research, of which its flagship is the *Industrial Development Report*.

Its research has helped to inform its work in industrial policy, of which UNIDO has long been a strong proponent, and for which it has also produced analytical tools such as the Competitive Industrial Performance Index. UNIDO is also the source of the annual *Yearbook of Industrial Statistics*, to which a report on mining and utilities is being added.

Statistics

Within the UN and among other international organizations, UNIDO is entrusted with the exclusive responsibility for the compilation of data on industry in the developing and transition-economy countries. Together with the data it receives from the Organisation for Economic Co-operation and Development (OECD) for the developed countries, UNIDO produces the *International Yearbook of Industrial Statistics* which provides global coverage of manufacturing value added, numbers of enterprises, employment, industrial wages, input costs and capital formation for industrial sectors down to the International Standard Industrial Classification (ISIC) four-digit level.

The major challenge in compiling the *Yearbook* is obtaining complete and up-to-date numbers for each country. In practice, universal coverage is impossible because many countries do not conduct regular industrial surveys. (UNIDO provides technical assistance to the statistical offices of many of those that do not.) Also, the data are usually several years old by the time of compilation; for example, the 2010 edition of the *Yearbook* contains only partial data for 2006. Nevertheless, the data are a unique and valuable source of comparative information on industrialization both across countries and over time. As a complement to the *Yearbook*, UNIDO also produced in 2010 *World Statistics on Mining and Utilities* with coverage of 61 countries. Although data on these sectors had been collected over several years, this was the first time a global compilation had been produced. The extensive industrial database maintained by UNIDO also generates individual country briefs which can also be accessed from its website.[2]

Research

UNIDO has maintained a strong tradition of research on different aspects of industrialization, producing four types of output. Foremost is its flagship publication, the *Industrial Development Report*, which analyzes contemporary industrial development challenges in depth. Five reports have been produced since 2002 (see Table 3.1), the most recent examining how enterprises can realize the triple bottom-line of commercial, social and environmental objectives.

Second, UNIDO staff produce working papers on specific industrialization topics. Of the more than 20 staff papers written in 2009, several discussed the impact of the global economic downturn on industry in the developing countries. These papers often draw on UNIDO's large industrial database. Third, UNIDO produces country-specific policy papers. A recent example is the report on industrial policy in Mongolia, mentioned below. Fourth, UNIDO has developed a "world productivity database" which has been generally accessible since 2008. It covers 112 developing countries and covers the time period 1960–2000. Data include measures of total factor productivity growth, capital stock, employment, education and health, and are the basis of country studies—of which 15 have been produced so far—on industrial productivity performance.

Table 3.1 Recent UNIDO *Industrial Development Reports*

Year	Subject
2002/03	Competing through innovation and learning
2004	Industrialization, environment and the MDGs in Sub-Saharan Africa
2005	*Capability building for catching-up: historical, empirical and policy dimensions*
2009	Breaking in and moving up: new industrial challenges for the bottom billion and the middle-income countries
2011	Industrial energy efficiency for sustainable wealth creation: capturing environmental, economic and social dividends

Industrial competitiveness

UNIDO has developed methodologies to measure industrial competitiveness and performance.[3] One of the most frequently used indicators is the Competitive Industrial Performance Index (CIP), which captures the ability of countries to produce and export competitively (see Box 3.1). These methodologies are intended to be used by countries to assess their own performance as a basis for designing and implementing industrial policy, and UNIDO has devised a "strategic industrial intelligence for policy" program to help build local capacities. Central to the program is the creation and training of autonomous national implementation teams and industrial intelligence units within influential government agencies, well placed to undertake industrial diagnoses and guide policy-makers.

***Box 3.1* UNIDO's Competitive Industrial Performance (CIP) index**

UNIDO developed the CIP index in 2002 as a means of assessing and comparing industrial performance over time and among countries. The index is made up of four dimensions and six indicators:

a) *Industrial capacity* indicates a country's level of industrialization relative to its economic size. It is measured by manufacturing value added per capita.
b) *Manufactured export capacity* is one of the indicators of global competitiveness and is measured by manufactured exports per capita.
c) *Industrialization intensity* measures the role of manufacturing in the economy and the technological complexity of the sector. Two indicators are combined in a simple average: the share of manufacturing in gross domestic product (GDP), and the share of medium- and high-technology activities in manufacturing value added.
d) *Export quality* gauges the importance of exports in an economy and their technological sophistication. It is measured by the simple average of two indicators: the share of manufactured goods in total exports, and the share of medium- and high-technology products in total exports.

To arrive at the CIP, these four dimensions are given equal weight and added together. To standardize the indices, the highest country in the sample scores 1 while the lowest scores 0, with the rest of the sample distributed between them. In the 2005 rankings, Singapore was the highest

> with 0.890. The developing countries that scored relatively well included Hong Kong (China) with 0.500, Malaysia with 0.474, Thailand with 0.423 and China with 0.418.
> (UNIDO, *Industrial Development Report 2002–03* (Vienna: 2002), and *Industrial Development Report 2009* (Vienna: 2009))

UNIDO started implementation of this program in Latin America. In 2003 UNIDO launched its first industrial competitiveness program in Ecuador. It started with a training course on UNIDO's industry and trade competitiveness analysis for staff from the Ministry of Trade and Industry (MICIP), the Central Bank of Ecuador and the National Competitiveness Council (CNC). Analytical work prepared during the training was used as input for the *Industrial Competitiveness Report of Ecuador* the following year. A specialized technical unit for competitive intelligence was then established with UNIDO's help in MICIP. The Unit produced a second *Industrial Competitiveness Report*, as well as several sector and other studies. It also served as a source of analysis for chambers of commerce. By 2006, the unit had been integrated into the Ministry, providing its services, publications and data to a broader clientele within the private and public sectors. With no further financial assistance from UNIDO, which now plays only an advisory role, the unit continues its involvement in the refinement of industrial policy and the elaboration of specific programs. It contributed to the elaboration of the country's industrial policy for 2008–10, and the development of an implementation plan. The unit now produces biannual industrial competitiveness reports, value-chain analysis, sectoral briefs, and policy notes and it offers online access to industrial information and data through an "industrial observatory."

Paraguay has followed the Ecuador model, creating an intelligence unit in 2007. UNIDO helped with training and staffing the unit, which supports policy through the production of analytical reports. In Colombia, UNIDO has helped to strengthen existing industrial intelligence units and fostered inter-agency networking and cooperation in the country. The Ministry of Industry and Trade, the Department of National Planning, and the Institute of National Statistics combined to contribute to the elaboration of Colombia's first industrial competitiveness report. UNIDO's program in Latin America has resulted in an expanding network of technical units offering the opportunity for exchanges of staff, and for the sharing of experience.

The program has also started activities in sub-Saharan Africa. In Cameroon, UNIDO has helped to establish an industrial observatory and has trained staff from several ministries. One of the outcomes was a report on the industrial performance of the country. Similarly in Rwanda and the Gambia, training was conducted on the development and use of industry and trade competitiveness indicators leading to diagnostic reports on their manufacturing sectors. In Cape Verde, UNIDO has helped set up a competitiveness intelligence unit in the newly-established Centre of Strategic Policy. Unit staff have been trained on UNIDO's methodology and they produced the country's industrial competitiveness report for 2010 as well as being engaged in several value-chain studies.

UNIDO has worked in Vietnam on a project designed to support the Ministry of Industry and Trade in designing industrial policies. In 2010 UNIDO assisted the ministry to set up an inter-ministerial industrial competitiveness group to act as a think-tank on industrialization and competitiveness. Staff underwent training and are producing the country's first industrial competitiveness report. In Palestine, UNIDO implemented a project to strengthen the Palestinian Trade Centre, the Palestinian Federation of Industries and the Ministry of Economy to enable them to identify products and export markets that could enhance the growth of manufactured exports.

Industrial policy

Industrial policy is sometimes considered controversial for two very different reasons. The first is ideological. From the 1980s onwards, conservative economists in developed countries have been critical of industrial policy which they construe as undue interference by the state in market systems. Bureaucrats should not be allowed to direct business, runs the argument, since—among other hazards—they are as likely to choose losers as winners. These arguments have influenced the concerns of some governments over UNIDO's own mandate. Experience has nevertheless demonstrated that both developed and developing countries have sought to influence the nature and direction of industrialization throughout the post-war period. In the case of many successful developing countries, industrial policy has been the essential basis of their advancement, as discussed in the Introduction. When the economies of the developed countries were derailed by a financial crisis in 2007–08, the cause was too little government regulation, rather than too much. The same countries then indulged in expensive industrial bail-outs to facilitate recovery. Industrial policy is not always successful, however, and it can commit resources to futile ends. When countries set their course, therefore, they need to do so with full knowledge of the options and their consequences. UNIDO's role can be a delicate one. Against a background of ideological skepticism from the developed countries, the organization needs to be best in class in terms of the quality of its expertise.

The second reason for the sensitivity of the subject derives from national sovereignty, since industrial policy is at the heart of all country development strategies. Developing countries divide into those that have remained wide open to policy advice, which in the case of many low-income countries has been dominated by the agendas of the Washington institutions, and those that have devised their own industrial strategies with selective external influence. In general, the industrialization record of the latter category has been much more successful, demonstrating the crucial importance of ownership. A prime example would be Singapore. In 1960 it received two industrial planning missions from the UN which helped to inspire the creation of industrial estates, on which the country's prosperity has been based, with limited further external advice.[4]

The policy paper that guides UNIDO's work in promoting private-sector development refers to two particular features of the new industrial policy: a recognition of market (as well as government) failures, and its normative character.[5] Market failure calls for policies that can correct distortions and permit the market to work more effectively. UNIDO talks of information failures and coordination failures. To succeed, particularly in open economies, entrepreneurs need information about cost structures and about their relative competitiveness. Governments can obtain and provide such information as a public good for the private sector. Coordination failures derive from a lack of infrastructure and diseconomies of scale. Building infrastructure is not an exclusive state concern, but can result from productive partnerships between the public and private sectors. Other solutions to the coordination problem are the clustering of enterprises, which states can facilitate (see Chapter 4).

There are also normative concerns of policy. Markets are concerned with bottom lines, but commercial viability does not always coincide with wider development objectives. Enhancing the competitiveness of certain sectors can raise productivity and incomes, but can have polarizing consequences for society more broadly. A manifestation of this process is the exacerbation of income inequalities as economies grow. Policy can help to ensure that industrialization is more inclusive. There are also market failures associated with environmental degradation. The planetary scale of concerns such as adverse climate change also point to the urgent need for public intervention.

Evolving models

Traditionally, views on industrial policy have differed according to perceptions of the role of the state. The "minimalist" school has the state playing a role that is generally supportive of the private industrial sector, but neutral with respect to preferences for individual sectors. In the "maximalist" school, the state's role is more preponderant, with an intent to influence the composition of industry, favoring some sectors over others and sponsoring the emergence of new areas of activity.

The Introduction referred to an evolution in the approach. Industrial policy may fail in its objectives, or be wrongly pursued, but failure can be a basis for learning. Some analysts have proposed a new way of thinking about industrial policy within the last few years.[6] Instead of a dichotomous minimal-maximal approach, "new" industrial policy perceives the role of the state as "process-oriented, multi-stakeholder-driven, flexible and open-ended" to cite the most recent UNIDO policy paper.[7] Dani Rodrik has spoken about a more organic "discovery" process whereby government, business and all relevant stakeholders learn from each other about costs and opportunities through a process of consultation, leading to appropriate and acceptable decisions about industrialization. Central to UNIDO's approach is the recognition that "the private sector is the main driver of employment generation and growth."[8]

UNIDO's "strategic" industrial policy approach is defined as government interventions "aimed at steering economic activity, particularly the intra- and inter-sectoral structure of production, towards areas that are expected to offer better prospects for economic growth than would be the case in the absence of such interventions."[9] Three types of industrial strategy may be distinguished. In the first place, diversification, which means broadening the industrial base by nurturing wholly new manufacturing activities. This is inter-industry structural change. Second, expansion and upgrading: focusing on existing manufacturing activities while encouraging capacity expansion, and an upgrading of products, processes and functions (intra-industry structural change). Third, deepening, which involves creating more backward and forward linkages and complementarities within one industry (intra-industry structural change).

Policy principles

Contemporary literature, as well as the analysis and experience of UNIDO and other organizations and their programs, suggests a number of principles to guide strategic industrial policymaking.

Ownership

Local stakeholders need to own and direct the industrial policymaking process in order to create the necessary mutual understanding and learning among all actors involved in industrial strategizing. UNIDO's role is therefore to act as an external agent which facilitates, but does not prescribe, the required interactions.

No "one-size-fits-all"

Structural change is very specific to context and not amenable to standardized policy solutions. National and regional circumstances are of relevance. Based on available evidence, and drawing on existing industrialization experiences, a clear understanding is needed of what works and what does not. Trial and error play an important part in policymaking, and research is helpful into new economic activities, and the identification of underlying cost structures.

Supporting and challenging

The government's role is both supportive and adjudicative. It needs to assist the private sector in exploring cost structures and identifying new products. In addition to supporting entrepreneurs in their search for diversification and upgrading, however, the government must also judge the economic feasibility of new projects and be ready to terminate support where necessary, implying the existence of a capable reform team, but also the need again for trial and error. The picking-winners approach has been criticized in the past because of the persistence of governments in supporting some infant industries which were always destined to become commercial failures. Thus, entrepreneurs need to be aware that government support is time-limited and performance-based. Non-performers and rent-seekers should not continue indefinitely to be on the government's books. As Rodrik puts it, "uncertainty ensures that even optimal policies will lead to mistakes. The trick is for governments to recognize those mistakes and withdraw support before they become too costly."[10]

Impact

While impact cannot be ensured, limited resources in developing countries mean that strategic industrial policymaking should concentrate on interventions that are most likely to achieve lasting effects. Four aspects are important.

In the first place, government intervention needs to identify and target specific constraints. Market failure—such as the inability of the price system to reflect future scarcities—is one, but anything that appears to be holding back structural change needs to be targeted. Second, there need to be managerial and technological capabilities available to design and implement policies and to ensure that they generate a self-reinforcing dynamic. Third, the economic feasibility of a sector or activity must be scrutinized. It is important to establish feasible rates of improvement, anticipate the evolution of demand, and estimate the cost-benefit ratio of government support for alternative options. Risk assessment should also be part of the scrutiny. Finally, decisions should be evidence-based, supported by sufficient research, and based on a range of views and options. Interventions should be subject to continuous review and independent third-party evaluation.

Policies in practice

Implementation should also invoke good-practice principles. One is the provision of indirect rather than direct support. On the one-to-one-to-many principle, competent service providers should be helped to support enterprises, rather than UNIDO assisting the individual enterprises themselves. Another recommended practice is co-financing by users. Having users pay for services encourages improvements in service quality and accountability. It also prevents crowding out of commercial providers by subsidized programs and increases the efficiency of resource allocation. Users will only buy those services for which they actually see a demand.

In 2010 UNIDO assisted Mongolia with a strategic review of its industrial policy. The country is the source of many unprocessed minerals and commodities and, having a small domestic market, is reliant on their export. The country produces more than 80 valuable minerals ranging from copper to crude oil as well as cashmere, yak hair, sheep's wool, camel hair and red meat. With a small manufacturing sector accounting for just over 4 percent of GDP, and employing fewer than 50,000 people out of a total workforce of 1 million, there is substantial scope for developing higher value-added through the transformation of minerals and other commodities, leading to the creation of more jobs and incomes, and helping the country to iron out the shocks of volatile global raw material markets. The objective of the review was to assist the government to develop an industrial strategy to maximize the development returns from the growth of a viable manufacturing sector.

56 *Research and policy*

A UNIDO team worked in collaboration with public and private stakeholders in Mongolia. They assessed the current status of the manufacturing sector and compared its performance with countries in similar conditions (e.g. Botswana and Uruguay), proposing some new areas for the country to develop a comparative advantage. The resulting strategy is designed to improve manufacturing performance through higher-quality products, and to promote Mongolian products in specific global markets.

Another example comes from Iraq, where UNIDO has been collaborating with the UN Development Programme (UNDP) and the International Labour Organization (ILO) to promote private-sector development. Traditionally, the country's economic governance was highly centralized around major state enterprises with a limited role being played by the private sector. During the period of initial reconstruction, conditions were inimical to the generation of jobs and growth through private enterprise, and the program aims to improve the institutional environment—legal, regulatory, policy and administrative—to facilitate the emergence of a vibrant entrepreneurial sector over the long run. UNIDO's role is four-fold: it will undertake a comprehensive assessment of the country's legislative and institutional needs, building capacities for policymaking for enterprise development; strengthen the capacities of business development services and non-bank financial institutions; support local institutions in formulating local "economic recovery" strategies; and undertake pilot projects.

Conclusion

In its early days, when the whole subject of UN involvement in industrialization was contentious, UNIDO's work was as an original purveyor of ideas and research. Today, apart from its role as the generator of industrial and mining statistics, UNIDO's research and policy activities are far from unique. Research and advice on industrialization flow copiously from many sources, including from other international public organizations (such as the World Bank) and private consultancies. As the debate on industrial policy continues its lively course, UNIDO's voice is becoming inevitably smaller and in common with all the UN development organizations, UNIDO's research and policy advocacy lacks the financial clout of the multilateral development banks.

Its claims of comparative advantage in the policy arena, therefore, are based on its being perceived as a trusted partner by many developing country governments. It could make two other claims. Linking its research and policy advocacy more closely to the experience of practical industrialization processes should enrich its research and policy thinking. As a development organization, UNIDO's research has helped to advance its own thinking on the broader benefits of industrialization, and its capacity to address goals of poverty reduction, the subject of the next chapter.

A bigger question remains, however, on the role of UNIDO as a global forum. In the 1970s UNIDO was seen as a key mouthpiece of the industrial interests of the South. This was the era of the debate on the new international economic order and the role of UNIDO was quite distinctive, even if the eventual dividends for the developing countries were meager. Since that time, many other forums have emerged, mostly outside the UN, where economic issues are discussed. To remain relevant, UNIDO therefore needs to continue re-making and re-discovering its role as convener, supplementing inter-governmental deliberations with forums comprising other influential stakeholders, leading to outcomes that impact industrial policy and practice. This point is revisited in Chapter 7.

4 Poverty reduction through productive activities

- The value-chain
- Entrepreneurship development
- Building e-competence
- Location, location, location: the importance of clusters
- Export consortia
- Agri-business
- Investment promotion and the business environment
- Technology promotion
- Conclusion

Poverty reduction only came into the common language of UN development in the 1980s, and before the UN Development Programme (UNDP) produced its first *Human Development Report* in 1990, the human dimensions of development were largely absent from the objectives of individual organizations and agencies. Many, including UNIDO, subscribed to more technocratic approaches which assumed that industrial (or agricultural or trade or other sectoral aspects of) development was their principal objective. Neither of the detailed Danish-sponsored diagnoses of UNIDO during the 1990s (see Chapter 1) mentioned poverty as an organizational priority, and it did not feature in the "business plan" that helped to re-launch the organization in 1997.

At the UN summit of 2000, however, the endorsement of the Millennium Development Goals (MDGs) enshrined human development outcomes—and within them income poverty reduction as goal number one—as principal objectives of the system. Many organizations, including UNIDO, then began to make poverty reduction a principal focus of their activities. For UNIDO, this was in answer to the questions: industrial development for what? and for whom? One upshot of this new emphasis on the human dimension was a major research project called Combating Marginalization and Poverty through Industrial

Development (COMPID), which began in 2002. UNIDO's subsequent annual reports give prominence to the poverty-alleviating impacts of UNIDO projects, with poverty reduction explicitly mentioned in mission statements and organizational objectives.

The change ran deeper than mere semantics. A more concentrated attention to broader human development results is part of what distinguishes the UN system. Externally, it was important to tell the development story. Thus when UNIDO re-wrote its mission statement after the Millennium Summit, it recast its first objective in terms of poverty reduction. This reformulation was important in conveying the human dimension of UNIDO's work, but was not intended to imply that poverty concerns were confined to one objective. Internally, therefore, the change meant a more careful consideration of human outcomes in the design and execution of every project, under each of the main priorities. This emphasis is still true today.

An important word in the new mission statement is "inclusive." The increasingly competitive global economy can create and exacerbate inequalities, both among countries and within them. UNIDO has brought the focus of its activities to bear on the countries that are at risk of being left behind in the globalization process, and in particular the Least Developed Countries (LDCs) and the countries of Africa. Within countries, it is also the poorer and marginalized who are targeted and this chapter will also look at the activities of UNIDO in fostering new productive capacity in rural communities.

The next three chapters are concerned respectively with the three main priority themes of the organization, all of which are designed to respond to the poverty mandate. This chapter is mainly concerned with the first of these themes. It starts with a description of the industrial value-chain as a frame of reference for different types of technical intervention that can help enterprises to become more competitive. It describes country, regional and global initiatives that seek to support small entrepreneurs around the world, including through the application of new information and communication technologies. The importance of enterprise clusters, touted as a key to raising the competitive advantage of small firms, is outlined. Export consortia are a special category of clusters, designed to help member companies to penetrate foreign markets successfully.

UNIDO has also recognized that much of its activity, particularly in Africa, revolves around what it describes as agri-business. This chapter goes on to describe in detail a major new program for the benefit of that continent which is lagging furthest behind in terms of manufacturing development, but where agro-processing offers growing potential.

Finally, the chapter describes UNIDO's long-established programs of investment and technology promotion. The first Investment and Technology Promotion Office (ITPO) was established in 1976 as a means of promoting North to South investment flows. The most recent have been set up in developing countries, reflecting the new directions of foreign direct investment (FDI) and technology transfer. The nature of UNIDO's work in this area has changed, leading to the development of new and different tools to guide investors.

The value-chain

UNIDO's assistance to the enterprise sector can be illustrated by reference to the industrial value-chain, of which a stylized version is shown in Figure 4.1. A value-chain comprises the complete range of transactions and support services required to bring a product from its origins to its end-use. Making value-chains work better, and within them, enhancing the efficiency and competitiveness of enterprises, particularly the smallest, is a way of describing UNIDO's broader development aims.

The diagram shows the various entry-points at which the activities of a development organization can make a difference. In the middle of industrial value-chains are the enterprises (producers). Each one can be made to work more productively and effectively through the adoption of good management, improved work practices, and a general upgrading of entrepreneurial skills, including e-competence. The domain of entrepreneurship development, indicated by the number 1 in the diagram, is the subject of the next two sections. (Chapter 6 deals with another aspect of enterprise efficiency: improving the energy use and environmental impacts of enterprises.)

The number 2 refers to the horizontal integration of enterprises, otherwise known as clustering or agglomeration. The benefits of this approach, and UNIDO's activities in the area, are the subject of the ensuing section. The section after that looks at agri-business, another key focus of UNIDO, and in value-chain terms, concerned especially with strengthening vertical integration (numbers 3 and 4). Number 5 is concerned with the domestic business environment, and the final sections look at UNIDO's activities in promoting inward FDI and technology promotion.

Entrepreneurship development

The business-development nexus has long been the subject of debate, and often controversy. In the 1970s the UN system, and the development

Poverty reduction through productive activities 61

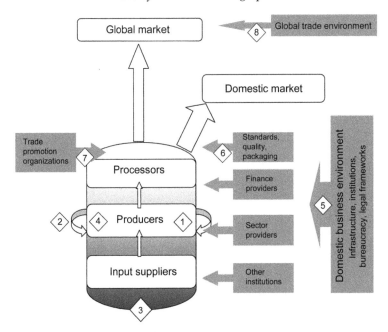

Figure 4.1 Industrial value-chain
Note: The diagram indicates the various ways in which competitiveness may be enhanced at different points on the chain:
[1] Enterprises can improve their production efficiency through increasing output per input and lowering production costs.
[2] Horizontal integration of enterprises, such as through the formation of producer groups or clusters of similar producers, can enhance economies of scale, create industry standards and encourage joint marketing.
[3] Closer vertical interaction, which involves contractual relationships up and down the chain among input suppliers, producers and processors can promote efficiencies.
[4] Value is also increased through functional upgrading, whereby producers undertake additional processing (e.g. from green coffee beans to roasting and grinding; from milk to other dairy products).
[5] Enterprises thrive in a healthy business environment, with well-functioning support institutions, efficient bureaucracy and infrastructure.
[6] Products can be upgraded by meeting higher quality standards.
[7] Better marketing is important, through improved packaging, better information on markets, advertising and attendance at trade fairs—often with the support of trade promotion organizations.
[8] At the international level, the global trading environment is influenced by market access conditions, including tariff and non-tariff measures.
Source: Adapted from Stephen Browne and Sam Laird, *The International Trade Centre* (London: Routledge, 2011), 8.

62 *Poverty reduction through productive activities*

community at large, identified the private sector with big business and the transnational corporations. The UN Centre on Transnational Corporations (UNCTC) perceived business through a predatory lens, and sought through research and technical assistance (TA) to assist developing countries to strike more favorable bargains in negotiations with transnational corporations (TNCs). The New York-based Centre was closed as an independent body in the 1980s and merged into the United Nations Conference on Trade and Development (UNCTAD) in Geneva, where it became a program to track FDI. With the emergence of Brazil, China and India and other emerging economies as major sources of FDI, this program has now taken on a stronger South-South dimension. FDI is seen as a more benign influence on development, and UNIDO itself has an active program of investment promotion (see below).

Big business has also come to be associated with corporate social responsibility (CSR) and development agencies have been able successfully to tap into private resources in support of their development programs. Again, UNIDO is no exception, and some examples of these partnerships are also discussed below. Thus, from a position of circumspection, the UN system has developed a more constructive relationship with business, seeking to encourage the private sector to adopt a more development-friendly stance. In 1999 the UN established a "global compact" which established 10 principles for businesses to sign up to in the areas of human rights, environment, employment and anti-corruption. Then in 2004 the UN convened a Commission on the Private Sector and Development, which prepared a report called *Unleashing Entrepreneurship: Making Business Work for the Poor.*[1] Again, the report was mainly about how business (particularly big business) could be of benefit to development.

These initiatives have tended to construe business as "creating value for the poor," as a UNDP report puts it.[2] The dynamics of this process can take various forms. The UN Global Compact—which now numbers over 6,000 businesses, the majority of them small and medium-sized—helps to raise the consciousness of businesses for their development impact. UNIDO is one of the six core UN agencies in the Compact.

However, there is also a much more fundamental meaning to the private sector-development nexus. From a focus on the public sector, development agencies have come round to an understanding that the vast majority of the poor in developing countries—the principal targets of development—are themselves the constituents of "business" and the private sector. They may be the poorest farmers or the heads of tiny enterprises, in the formal or informal sectors, but they are all striving to make a living by whatever means they have. The essential objectives of development, therefore, are to empower and support this vast constituency of mainly small businesses.[3] The World Bank's International Finance Corporation (IFC) has determined that there is a high correlation between the density of micro-enterprises and small and medium-sized enterprises (SMEs—numbers per 1,000 people) and national income levels.[4] So while business can work for the poor, it is even more vital that the poor be enabled to work as effective businesses.

SMEs (or MSEs—micro and small enterprises) are a central concern for UNIDO, which targets them as some of its primary beneficiaries. The Entrepreneurship and Skills Development Program focuses on women and youth entrepreneurship, particularly in rural areas, and entrepreneurship for creative industries.

Globally, UNIDO estimates that women make up one-quarter to one-third of the MSE business population in developing countries, and one-third in manufacturing. They are particularly predominant in food production, where they account for up to 80 percent of the labor force. However, they are held back by unequal access to productive resources and services, in particular finance and skills development. UNIDO seeks to help women overcome these disadvantages. A representative example comes from Morocco, where 400 women engaged in producing olive oil, fruit and vegetable drying, and textiles received training in management, good production practices and food safety, marketing and promotion. As a result, their sales have increased on the domestic and export markets and they have seen 40–50 percent increases in productivity and incomes. UNIDO also runs entrepreneurship training for youth, building on the facilities, where available, of vocational training centers. Many centers require substantial upgrading and revamped syllabuses. In Côte d'Ivoire 3,000 young people, women and ex-combatants have benefited from technical and managerial skill development at two rehabilitated and re-equipped centers. In Sudan three vocational training centers have been revived. Two of these are in the new country of South Sudan and the current projects are each aimed at training 2,000 youths in entrepreneurship skills.

UNIDO has also implemented entrepreneurship development programs for women and youth in agri-business in other African countries, including Eritrea, Kenya, Malawi, Tanzania and Zimbabwe. In the Mano River Union countries of West Africa—Côte d'Ivoire, Guinea, Liberia and Sierra Leone—where unemployment rates among youth range up to nearly 90 percent, UNIDO is collaborating with the International Labour Organization (ILO) and UNDP in promoting "decent" work. High unemployment is partly a consequence of recent conflict in the region, with many ex-combatants without work. The program helps young people to devise and implement their own community and business projects, obtaining on-the-job training and sharing their knowledge and skills.

UNIDO's support to enterprises can be illustrated with reference to two ongoing global programs: in creative industries and in the manufacture of essential drugs.

Creative industries

Creative industries refer to the cycle of creation, production and marketing of tangible goods and intangible services that use creativity and intellectual capital as primary inputs. As UNIDO defines them, creative industries encompass heritage, art and crafts, and media as well as innovations and product development in agri-business, including textiles, leather, wood, and traditional food items.

In Bhutan UNIDO has helped in the mapping of the country's cultural resources, strengthened vocational training and business support institutions, and developed entrepreneurial competence programs. In China the targets are the recognized ethnic minorities who make up 8 percent of the population but are disproportionately represented among the country's poor. In four provinces UNIDO is assisting in empowering ethnic groups by managing their cultural resources in lucrative ways, including and especially through tourism. In Egypt, where date production is a profitable activity, the focus of activity has been on the rest of the plant crop rather than the fruit itself. UNIDO has helped to promote those parts of the palm used to produce a line of traditional household items.

Essential drugs

Some 30 percent of the world's population lack access to life-saving pharmaceutical drugs, and in some African and Asian countries the proportion is 50 percent.[5] The three most deadly diseases in the world are HIV/AIDS, with which 40 million people are infected, tuberculosis, from which 2 million die every year, and malaria, which kills 2.7 million. Access to drugs to treat these and other diseases and illnesses is inhibited by high prices, which are driven up by the monopoly power of intellectual property rights. Trade in medicines is governed by the Trade-Related Aspects of Intellectual Property Rights (TRIPS) agreement of the World Trade Organization (WTO), which prevents companies from making, selling or trading patented medicines for a period of 20 years. However, TRIPS allows some exceptions, and patented drugs can be produced in the case of serious public health needs and epidemics, under licensing arrangements.

In 2006 UNIDO began implementing a program to support developing countries in strengthening their capacity for the manufacture of essential drugs. In a first phase, several Least Developed Countries were examined, but none of their enterprises met the minimum eligibility standards for upgrading. The project then chose companies in Algeria, Brazil, Jordan, Palestine, and South Africa as its principal focus, adopting a comprehensive approach which encompassed policy, skills training and enterprise development. Enterprises were required to meet Good Manufacturing Practices (GMP) standards and achieve World Health Organization (WHO) pre-qualification.

On one plane—the strengthening of productive capacity—the project has been successful, even if production has had to be confined mainly to middle-income countries. On another plane—that of meeting poverty and MDG goals—the outcomes are more difficult to gauge. As a 2010 evaluation puts it, "there is no information on whether or not, and under what conditions, domestic production of pharmaceuticals actually makes a meaningful contribution to access and affordability of essential medicines to patients who need them most."[6] The principle of "if you build it they will come" does not apply if domestic production augments supply, but is not able to reduce costs sufficiently to make the drugs affordable to poorer communities.

Building e-competence

Information and communication technologies (ICTs) have opened up many opportunities for SMEs (and MSEs) all over the world. ICTs are tools for the acquisition, storage and dissemination of information. They enhance efficiency and speed up business processes. They link MSEs with markets everywhere, including the most distant, and they connect enterprises to business services and sources of finance. The existence of accessible ICTs has itself led to the creation of many new SMEs.

In many developing countries, however, the extraordinary potential of ICTs remains largely unrealized and UNIDO's assistance is aimed at overcoming the existing obstacles. The first challenge is affordable access. In 2009, according to the International Telecommunication Union (ITU), the cost of a fixed broadband connection in developed countries was US$28 per month, as against $190 per month in developing countries (purchasing power parity basis). Among developing countries there are also wide variations however, and in some the costs range much higher. In Africa, the costs of broadband are on average three times higher than in Asia.[7] These cost variations account for the differences in broadband penetration in 2010, from 23.8 subscriptions per 100 inhabitants in Europe, to 5.5 in Asia, 1.9 in the Arab States and only 0.2 in Africa. A second obstacle is computer familiarity. In all developing regions, many people lack basic ICT literacy and computing skills. A third problem relates to content. What can be obtained online is often of limited suitability or relevance to the needs of aspiring micro-entrepreneurs.

UNIDO's programs in e-competence are founded on Business Information Centers (BICs), which aim to overcome these obstacles by providing common ICT facilities to multiple users. BICs are usually public-private ventures and they cater to the needs of SMEs by offering advisory services to entrepreneurs, reliable internet connections, training in ICT applications, access to business information, and connections to potential markets. These BICs operate under certain principles, however, the most important of which are respect for the specific circumstances and needs of local populations, openness to female entrepreneurs, and business models to ensure sustainability and replicability.

Mobile telephony has spread much more rapidly than computer use and internet connectivity. In 2010 there were 70 mobile phone subscriptions per 100 inhabitants in developing countries as a whole, with 69 in Asia and 45 in Africa.[8] To increase the number of beneficiaries, especially in more remote communities, UNIDO is attempting to link more people to the services of the BICs through their mobile phones.

Under its Business Partnership Program, UNIDO has developed ties with several ICT-related multinational companies. Two of the most successful have been with Microsoft and Hewlett-Packard. In Uganda UNIDO helped to develop a network of BICs in eight districts in different parts of the country. It joined forces with Microsoft's Unlimited Potential program to help meet local needs for hardware and software, including in the BICs. The partners launched the Uganda Green Computer Company in order to refurbish second-hand equipment and provide training in ICT. The company is commercially sustainable. It disassembles personal computer hardware, salvages the working parts, and re-assembles the parts into usable PC equipment with genuine (non-pirated) software. The equipment is then re-sold for less than half the cost of new PCs. In the process, unused parts are disposed of in environmentally responsible ways. The partnership has also helped to tailor UNIDO's entrepreneurial training modules to use in BICs.

UNIDO has also partnered with Hewlett-Packard's Learning Initiative for Entrepreneurs (HP LIFE) program and the Education Development Center to teach business and IT solutions in marketing, operations, communications and finance. The curriculum has been developed by the Swiss-based Micro-Enterprise Acceleration Institute (MEA-I) and folded into UNIDO's own Entrepreneurship Curriculum Program. The UNIDO-LIFE partnership has established over 90 centers in 13, mostly middle- and high-income, countries (Algeria, Brazil, China, Egypt, India, Kenya, Morocco, Nigeria, Saudi Arabia, South Africa, Tunisia, United Arab Emirates and Uganda), and claims to have certified 270 trainers and trained a total of 42,000 students.

Location, location, location: the importance of clusters

In some important respects, the information revolution and the advent of modern ICTs have made geography less relevant. Many small and micro enterprises, particularly in the services sectors, have sprung up and are thriving in remote parts of some developing countries because modern technologies have helped to connect them to distant sources and markets— a prospect which had never been previously open to them.

However, globalization and a shrinking planet have also underlined the importance of another geographical dimension: the phenomenon of enterprise clustering or agglomeration, the potential advantages of which have been touted for some time.[9] Michael Porter's seminal work highlighted the advantages of clustering for the competitiveness of sectors and whole countries,[10] and as value-chains develop and extend across frontiers, clustering has become an important consideration for industrial policy because of the competitive advantages of scale (see the Introduction to this volume).

Clustering of similar or complementary enterprises can favor performance in several ways. Clustered enterprises can be more competitive than single (isolated) firms because they benefit from collective efficiency gains. These gains, or "external economies" include the development of a local specialized labor force, access to common suppliers of key inputs and machinery, and shared information about operations, innovations, marketing opportunities and other key sources of value to the sector. Strength also comes from collective representation, and clusters stand to benefit more from the services of support institutions and professional associations, as well as from favorable public policies.

There is also evidence that successful clustering spurs growth. This is consistent with Porter's finding that greater competition stimulates innovation and productivity and favors expansion of production. There are some spectacular examples. One city in China (Qiaotou) began as a cluster of village enterprises and has grown to become the supplier of two-thirds of all garment buttons in the world.[11] Another Chinese city supplies most of the socks worn today.

However, does this growth help reduce poverty? Again the evidence appears positive. UNIDO has found that successful clusters are not just extended production facilities, but can act as socio-economic systems which are meshed with local communities:

> Not only do entrepreneurs and workers share a similar social, cultural and political background, but also norms of reciprocity and collective practices of self-help are common among employers and employees. Overall, this accounts for a distribution of the benefits of growth that is likely to be more inclusive than in other economic systems.[12]

Clusters are good in principle, therefore, but practice is far from ideal. Enterprises working in proximity may compete or complement and UNIDO uses a word "co-optition" to imply that both may apply in some circumstances. However, there is not always a natural propensity for them to seek out the benefits of successful clustering. Locally, there may be a lack of trust which hampers interaction, and an absence of professional associations or other institutions that could facilitate dialogue. The population of an inchoate cluster may consist of one or more large dominant companies (which may be foreign-owned). They attract the exclusive attention of support institutions and crowd out the interests of other small enterprises.

UNIDO does not create industrial clusters, but it can help to make them work better. As a neutral non-commercial organization, it is well-placed to mediate the different interests in a cluster and promote cooperation. UNIDO uses brokers, known as cluster development agents (CDAs), to work with cluster communities. They provide broadly three types of service: building trust and mechanisms of governance within clusters themselves; strengthening the capacities of local institutions which can support clusters; and giving a developmental (pro-poor) orientation to clusters. These services are described below and illustrated by reference to examples in Box 4.1.

Successful cooperation is based on trust, and trust is sustained by appropriate institutions of governance. These institutions include organizations, networking schemes, as well as norms and values that can foster collaboration and joint action. CDAs help to discover the best mechanisms for the governance of each cluster, propose the forms of representation and interaction, and encourage contracts, statutes and collaborative agreements which can ensure compliance with the collective interests of the members.

Clusters are not only "horizontal" agglomerations. Within value-chains there are important vertical linkages, whether backwards to suppliers, or forwards to processors and buyers. These vertical value- or supply-chains feature strongly in UNIDO's activities in agri-business (next section) and for the success of clustered enterprises in general. UNIDO encourages stronger links along the supply-chain, through buyer-seller arrangements between producers and buyers, sub-contracting, and in helping to ensure conformity with standards and product quality.

UNIDO also helps to enhance the capacities of support institutions, both in the public and private sectors. These include all providers of business development services: technical institutes, industry and professional associations, academic bodies and private firms. The assistance can range from skills training to advisory services, to facilitating access to services already available.

Clusters help to consolidate and strengthen the position of enterprises in supply-chains, but the objectives of cluster initiatives are not confined to efficiency and productivity. The role of a development organization like UNIDO is to identify clusters that can generate economic opportunities for the poor, and to do so inclusively, especially for the benefit of women and the marginalized. Pro-poor approaches imply labor-intensive and low-capital solutions based often on artisanal skills. Beyond the technical and commercial considerations, there are concerns of empowerment, representation and voice, which are central in overcoming poverty.

Box 4.1 provides three representative examples of the benefits of clustering. The first example, from Nicaragua, illustrates the importance of the CDA's role in encouraging a business services organization to support a cluster. The Ethiopian example shows how clustering encouraged a major engineering company to exercise corporate social responsibility in providing training to its SME suppliers. In the Indian example, women were brought out of their homes and enabled to play a larger role, not merely within the cluster, but also in a wider societal context, developing their own self-help schemes.

Box 4.1 **Assistance to industrial clusters in Nicaragua, Ethiopia and India**

Nicaragua

Rivas has 4,000 banana producers, mostly small-scale enterprises selling to the local or regional market. About 500 producers are affiliated to an association providing enterprise development services to its members, called (by its Spanish acronym) APLARI. When UNIDO started assisting the cluster, the CDA determined that APLARI could play a key role in cluster development, given its large membership, the legitimacy it enjoyed in the cluster and its proven implementation capacity.

To bolster its capacity to play this role, the CDA trained three of APLARI's staff in the cluster development methodology. They were taken on study-tours to witness other clusters that were performing well and given continuing support. The CDA also helped APLARI to identify other local and national institutions that were involved in cluster strengthening to enlist their support.

APLARI then took control of the process and facilitated the establishment of working groups, including representatives of the relevant institutions and cluster entrepreneurs. Individual entrepreneurs were in charge of coordinating one or more cluster development activities. By the end of the project, the informal working groups had coalesced into a permanent cluster commission with constituent members, including APLARI, who were representatives of all cluster actors. The commission is linked through a network to other local and national institutions. In taking a leading role in formulating and assisting the implementation of joint activities, APLARI has helped to ensure that the benefits of the cluster are spread amongst all stakeholders.

Ethiopia

The city of Mekelle in the Tigray National Regional State is home to a metal and woodworking cluster, comprising more than 250 metal and wood workshops and 24 cooperative associations. Most of the workshops manufacture household equipment, office furniture, agricultural implements, construction materials, and simple machines. Mekelle also hosts one of the largest manufacturers of metal products in Ethiopia, Mesefin Industrial Engineering (MIE), one of the largest equipment manufacturing and industrial engineering companies in East Africa. (Mekelle has also been included in the Millennium Cities Initiative of Columbia University, New York, through which UNIDO has assisted in mobilizing incoming foreign investment.)

The cluster experienced rapid growth in the early part of the last decade, boosted by public procurement contracts and growing demand for machinery accompanying a boom in agricultural production. MIE also started providing subcontracting arrangements to a few metal workshop enterprises. The cluster then went into decline. Demand fell, but in addition, the smaller enterprises had growing difficulties in meeting quality requirements and they were excluded from participating in tenders and public procurement. Poor product quality also led to a decline in orders from MIE.

To help the cluster regain competitiveness, UNIDO set up a working group, which included representatives of the SMEs, MIE, and local institutions including the University of Mekelle and the Bureau of Trade, Industry and Transportation (BOTIT). The working group led to enhanced communications within the cluster. It discussed common problems and led to a revival of the subcontracting agreements with MIE. A shared development strategy was devised, under which MIE is providing training within its facilities to SMEs in welding, drawing, design and quality control, with support and co-funding from BOTIT. In addition, the University of Mekelle is collaborating with MIE on the development of new prototypes of machinery that can be manufactured using locally available inputs. Designs formulated by the College of Engineering are tested by MIE, which then undertakes production, subcontracting the manufacturing of small metal and wooden parts and tools to SMEs. Finally BOTIT, which is a government agency, facilitates the participation of micro- and small-scale firms in tenders for public procurement and provides collective working premises. Through these collaborative agreements the cluster has produced 24 new machine prototypes which can substitute for previously imported machinery. SMEs in the cluster are again benefiting from more stable market conditions.

India

In Barpalli there is a cluster of hand-loom weavers. Women have played a key part in the cluster, being fully involved in pre-loom activities. However, they were confined to their homes, had a marginal influence on the activities of the cluster and had no control over the household income that they had earned. Through a UNIDO project, the women established their own representative grouping, or federation. The federation organized social activities, including literacy camps, and helped to build greater self-confidence among the women, bringing them greater recognition in the eyes of their male partners. Once their confidence had increased, UNIDO facilitated their fuller participation in the economic life of the cluster. Various other benefits followed. The members of the federation started their own microfinance scheme, saving their incomes and extending loans to members in financial distress who would otherwise have gone to informal moneylenders. The federation has also taken on training schemes for its members in areas of self-management, leadership development and finance. Subsequently, the women have started to undertake weaving activities with the federation providing them with more sophisticated services such as design, product development and marketing.

Export consortia

For SMEs in developing countries access to external markets can be important to their growth and development. Export consortia are a special category of cluster, not necessarily characterized by location and close proximity, which promote the export of goods produced by their members through joint actions. Export consortia can achieve many of the benefits of clustering described above, but in addition a pooling of efforts by the members of a consortium enhances export marketing skills, including the identification of export destinations, knowledge of buyer preferences, understanding and achieving quality standards and the appointment of buyers and distributors. Attaining and maintaining an adequate volume of exports is also easier when enterprises in consortia are able to offer a complete range of related products. One of UNIDO's first projects in promoting export consortia was in Morocco. Since 2004, working with the government and the Moroccan Exporters' Association, UNIDO has helped in the formation of 20 consortia involving 150 enterprises in nine different production sectors. All the consortia have worked on developing their promotional tools (with leaflets, catalogues and websites) and participated in trade exhibitions and commercial missions. They have negotiated preferential terms with local service providers and financial institutions. Apart from production modernization and upgrading, some have organized shared training facilities.

As an example of productive public-private partnership—essential for any successful exporting campaign—the Moroccan Government has established a fund to support the promotional activities of consortia. The main trade promotion organization (Maroc Export) and the agency for SME development (ANPME) provide them with special assistance. The consortia claim success in terms of export performance. A textile and garment group has seen its exports grow twice as fast as the national average, and a consortium of travel agencies has grown to be the third largest tour operator in the country.

Another example of facilitating market access for SMEs, through supplier development, comes from Egypt. In 2009 UNIDO established a partnership with the METRO Group of Germany, the world's fourth largest retailer, to buy produce from 90 SMEs and 800 farmers along the Nile valley. UNIDO had already been working with some of these suppliers, encouraging them to form clusters and upgrade the quality and safety of their produce. The partnership with METRO has expanded these benefits. Suppliers meet quality, safety and traceability[13] requirements, and adapt to consumer demand, while the buyer supports development projects that favor local communities and encourage sustainability.

After Egypt, UNIDO and METRO are expanding their partnership to suppliers of food and non-food products in several other countries, mostly in Asia and Africa. UNIDO also intends to partner with additional major buyers—retailers and manufacturers—in developed countries, encouraging them to tap into supplier consortia in developing countries.

Agri-business

The transformation of agriculture by adding value through agro-processing is a primary source of economic growth and income generation (see Introduction). Since three-quarters of the world's poor live in rural areas, most subsisting off agriculture, this transformation can be a principal means of tackling poverty.

***Box 4.2* Agro-definitions**

Agri-business: a broad concept that covers input suppliers, agro-processors, traders, exporters and retailers. Agri-business provides inputs to farmers and connects them to consumers through the financing, handling, processing, storage, transportation, marketing and distribution of agro-industry products.

Agro-industry: all the post-harvest activities that are involved in the transformation, preservation and preparation of agricultural production for intermediary or final consumption of food and non-food products. Agro-industry consists of six main manufacturing groups according to the International Standard Industrial Classification (ISIC): food and beverages; tobacco products; paper and wood products; textiles, footwear and apparel; leather products; and rubber products.

Agro-processing: the subset of manufacturing that processes raw materials and intermediate products derived from the agricultural sector. "Agro-processing industry" thus means transforming products originating from agriculture, forestry and fisheries.

(Kandeh K. Yumkella *et al.*, *Agribusiness for Africa's Prosperity* (Vienna: UNIDO, 2011), 28)

The potential is enormous. UNIDO estimates that barely 38 percent of agricultural production in developing countries undergoes any form of processing (against 98 percent in high-income countries). High-income countries, moreover, add nearly $185 of value by processing 1 ton of agricultural products, against only $40 in developing countries. Yet, this 38 percent generates 40–60 percent of manufactured value added in developing countries—nearly 70 percent in LDCs—and is the source of half their exports.[14] Historical data show that as development proceeds, and the relative size of the agricultural sector shrinks, the share of agro-industry rises.[15] Taking agri-business as a whole (agro-industry plus related services, see Box 4.2), it is a very important foundation of the industrialization process. However, some countries, particularly in Africa, are starting from a low base. The total value of agri-business in the sub-Saharan Africa region is no higher than that of Thailand, and a quarter that of Brazil. In all but two African countries (South Africa and Zimbabwe), the contribution of agriculture to gross domestic product (GDP) is higher than that of agri-business by 10 percentage points or more.[16]

The pivotal role of (the more broadly defined) agri-business provides the rationale for UNIDO's work in this area. However, accelerating the growth of agribusiness is not an end in itself. Most enterprises are links in a value-chain and where their position is a subordinate one, they lack bargaining power and lose rent to stronger partners. The setting of quality, safety, packaging and other standards—e.g. for food products—also bring challenges for the small enterprise, particularly where the ends of a chain are foreign consumers. The challenge for UNIDO is to ensure that, as agri-business takes hold, it can benefit as many enterprises as possible without marginalizing those that are smaller and more remote.

Because of its potential importance as a driver of pro-poor growth, the development of agri-business has a high priority for UNIDO, particularly in Africa. In 2011 it drew up its "seven pillars" of wisdom for agri-business, to serve as a set of guidelines.[17] These pillars have been derived from analysis of the constraints that agri-business development currently faces in Africa, and was highlighted by a 2008 meeting of the continent's ministers of industry, which drew up a Declaration on Accelerating Africa's Development through Industrialization.

Pillar 1: enhancing agricultural productivity

Agricultural production is the foundation and provides inputs to agro-industry. Modern technologies and techniques—including genetically modified crops and livestock—will be needed to boost agricultural growth and raise the productivity of the soil. These new farming approaches have been referred to as "sustainable intensification."[18]

Pillar 2: upgrading value-chains

For agri-business, value-chains begin with agricultural produce, and move through production and processing into packaging, marketing and sales, in domestic or international markets. For every product or service, value-chains include all of the enterprises involved in supplying, producing, processing and buying, as well as the organizations that provide the full range of supporting services: technical, business and financial. Building viable higher-value agri-business will depend increasingly on the capacity of enterprises to supply global, regional and local value-chains with products of a type and quality demanded by buyers. Along the chain, upgrading involves improvements in each link: products, processing, and enterprise management, as well as in supporting services and infrastructure.

Pillar 3: Exploiting demand

Markets rule. Whether production is for local or global consumption, it has to meet the quality and standards that buyers dictate. Globalization has helped to connect even the smallest enterprises of developing countries with foreign markets, bringing new opportunities, but also challenges of compliance with tastes and standards, and the vagaries of demand. International trade conditions also have a critical bearing on market opportunities. Tariff escalation for many products imported into developed countries effectively imposes a tax on agro-processing. While there are growing South-South market opportunities, tariffs remain high among developing countries for some products. Regional trade opportunities (especially within Africa) are also inhibited by tariff and non-tariff barriers and poor infrastructure (see Chapter 5).

Pillar 4: Strengthening technology and innovation

The most dynamic agro-industrial sectors in developing countries have demonstrated the importance of applying science, technology and innovation (STI). Most countries lack advanced training and research, but the right STI policies can help to ensure that agro-industry benefits from inputs from, and closer interaction with, national and international STI institutions.

Pillar 5: Promoting effective financing

All business requires supportive financing facilities, but in some countries agri-business development is perceived as high risk and unattractive.

Mobilizing both traditional and innovative sources of finance, however, is a key pillar. One of the challenges, therefore, is to present agro-industrial sectors as potentially progressive and profitable. Another is to supplement existing sources of financing with innovative mechanisms, including micro-finance and investment by diaspora.

Pillar 6: Creating a conducive business climate

No successful developing country has failed to create a domestic climate within which entrepreneurship can flourish. It starts with political stability and conducive and consistent policies of sound economic management, and includes favorable exchange rates, clear legal frameworks and supporting institutions for finance, packaging, marketing and infrastructure.

Pillar 7: Improving infrastructure and energy access

The commercial world has been transformed by new ICTs and they are now an essential part of any SME environment. Although shown to be commercially profitable at every income level, however, ICT penetration is still limited in some countries, and public policies need to facilitate wider access. Good physical infrastructure for land and maritime transportation is also still lagging in many developing countries and needs to be built or upgraded for effective supply and marketing. Energy access and assured power supplies are also of fundamental importance (see Chapter 6).

In agri-business UNIDO's services concentrate on four areas, addressed broadly to four or five of the above pillars. The first area is "techno-economic" advice. This is intended to provide countries with realistic options for the development of agro-industry, especially favoring small-scale enterprises. The advice includes technical feasibility studies, assessments of economic and environmental impact, as well as potential organizational linkages.

The second area is aimed at improving productivity and marketing. It builds capacity within individual product sectors by identifying and strengthening the services provided by specialized sectoral institutions and professional associations. These include design and technology centers to stimulate innovation. The third area goes down to the enterprise level. UNIDO can offer skills training and a range of services to improve the performance of individual enterprises, including marketing.

The fourth area is a more general one, which UNIDO puts under the rubric of "global forum." UNIDO can facilitate the participation of developing countries in the work of international organizations and conferences. More concretely, it prepares relevant training manuals and tool-kits, and collects and disseminates agro-industrial data as an input to decision-making. Examples of UNIDO's work in agro-industry are given in Box 4.3.

> **Box 4.3 UNIDO services to five agro-industrial product sectors**
>
> Food industry: since 2008 there have been growing concerns over food security as prices have risen worldwide and shortages of production and storage have emerged. Whatever the causes—population increase, changing consumer tastes, crop substitution—there is renewed urgency to increase the productivity of food crops, reduce post-harvest losses and introduce basic processing technologies to enhance food safety and preservation. UNIDO offers services in these areas, and one of the means of doing so is the establishment of food processing "pilot" centers. Centers have been created in Burkina Faso, Madagascar, Mali, Senegal, Tanzania and Uganda, and they are intended as a step toward a more modern food processing industry in these countries. They act as links in a chain, filling the space between farmers and market outlets. The centers help to improve the quality of produce, reduce post-harvest losses, foster basic processing and identify and deliver to markets. The goal is to add value to agricultural production and generate employment.
>
> Leather and products: Hides and skins are important by-products of the livestock sector and are available in abundant quantities in many developing countries. Leather products can be fashioned with relatively low capital investment and manufacturing is labor-intensive. However, tanning generates polluting effluents and can be damaging for the environment. UNIDO provides services to this sector along the whole processing cycle, from tanning to production, design and marketing, including the use of technologies and processes to minimize pollution.
>
> UNIDO also supports trade associations in this sector and has founded the Leather and Leather Products Industry Panel, a global network of technical agencies, government institutions, professional associations and private-sector representatives.
>
> Textiles and garments: With food, textile and garment producers employ the largest numbers in the manufacturing sector in low-income countries. There are some niche new markets in garment manufacturing which countries can aim to supply, but with so many suppliers worldwide, most production in the mainstream markets is highly competitive, particularly as

countries move up the value-chain from simple garment assembly to more vertically integrated processes. UNIDO supports developing countries in various ways, from the processing of natural fibers (especially cotton, silk, coir and jute) to product development and design, and marketing. UNIDO also helps in the introduction of technologies for modern techniques of computerized colorimetry, and assists enterprises in meeting higher environmental standards.

Wood and forest products: this is another product area where there is significant potential for upgrading in developing countries, where poor materials and design have traditionally hampered progress. UNIDO has a long record of assistance, and has made a specialty of the bamboo industry. Bamboo has many potentially useful, and hitherto under-utilized, applications. In India, which grows an estimated 30 percent of the world's bamboo, UNIDO has helped the agriculture ministry to create a cane and bamboo technology center in Assam which supports enterprises to develop skills and adopt technologies for bamboo processing. Products from bamboo include airplane "skins," desalination filters, diesel fuel, and medicine. Bamboo shoots provide food and bamboo can be turned into fiber for clothing, and used to reinforce concrete.

Agricultural machinery: mechanization is one of the keys to more productive and more competitive agriculture. In countries where the rural population is afflicted by diseases, including HIV/AIDS, mechanization can help to sustain production. UNIDO supports mechanized agriculture by assisting in the rehabilitation and maintenance of workshops which design and manufacture agricultural equipment and tools, and which repair and maintain machinery. It facilitates the acquisition of modern technologies by small businesses, helping to meet goals of productive employment and sound environmental management.

In agri-business, UNIDO works closely with other UN bodies, and in particular with the Food and Agriculture Organization (FAO) and the International Fund for Agricultural Development (IFAD). In joint projects UNIDO aims to contribute to the continuum from farm to consumer. In 2010 UNIDO, FAO and IFAD co-hosted the Conference on the Development of Agri-business and Agro-industry in Africa, in Abuja, Nigeria, at which governments signed up to the Abuja Declaration. The Declaration launched the African Agro-industry and Agri-business Development Initiative (3ADI), which helped to draw attention to the need to give more priority to African agriculture in the light of impending global food shortfalls. The program launched by the Declaration is designed to provide assistance in four areas: development of enabling policies and creation of public goods; enhancement of value-chain skills and use of technologies; strengthening of post-production institutions and services; and the reinforcement of financing and risk mitigation mechanisms. The program is mainly, but not exclusively, aimed at African countries (of which there are 10) and includes Afghanistan and Haiti. The three agencies have first ascertained the commitments of the host governments to mobilize resources for implementation of the program. They have subsequently identified one or more product sectors in each country and determined how to support them in creating productive and profitable value-chains.

Investment promotion and the business environment

FDI brings new skills and technologies. Through supplier relationships and sub-contracting, FDI can bring domestic enterprises into global markets, adding an international dimension to industrial value-chains. Exposure to global markets requires exacting levels of product quality, productive capacity and delivery schedules and can drive the process of technology upgrading, skill development and innovation.

The continual search by multinational companies for lower production costs and improved delivery has brought rapidly expanding opportunities to developing countries striving to build their industrial sectors. However, FDI also presents major competitive challenges. Many developing and transition-economy countries have improved their local business environments by liberalizing their regulatory regimes and introducing investment incentives, but not all have been successful in attracting FDI, nor in seeing from it development benefits. Even those that have succeeded have seen enclaves and growth areas develop, leading to wider spatial inequalities. Some FDI, especially in sub-Saharan Africa, has grown strongly in the extractive sectors of oils, gas and minerals creating new infrastructure and boosting foreign exchange, but these investments rarely form linkages with domestic suppliers, create limited numbers of local jobs and may detract from social and environmental development in the receiving countries.

UNIDO has worked with several countries to help improve their investment and business climate. A successful ongoing example is in Vietnam (see Box 4.4). Its promotion of "good" investment and technology, which can bring maximum benefits to the domestic economy and, above all, contribute to human development and poverty reduction, is much older and dates back to the earliest days of the organization. It has both external and internal dimensions, insofar as it works with current and prospective foreign investors to determine and channel their interests, while it also seeks to encourage the development of domestic institutions which can help to attract investors.

> **Box 4.4 Improving the business environment in Vietnam**
>
> *Vietnam: business registration*
>
> A conducive business environment unencumbered by bureaucracy and enjoying low transaction costs encourages prospective entrepreneurs and investors to enter markets. In Vietnam a 1999 UNIDO-Ministry of Planning and Investment (MPI) study highlighted the obstacles to company registration. It recommended the creation of specialized business registration offices, and a central computerized enterprise register easily accessible to the public. From 2000 the first offices were established, but it still took 50 days to obtain a business registration certificate following submission of a fully compliant registration dossier. Enterprises also had to separately register for a tax code, and obtain and register a seal-carving permit. In 2005 UNIDO assisted the MPI to lead the formulation of the country's first SME Development Plan 2006–10 through a consultative process involving many public and private entities. The Plan included a vertically integrated system of business registration; a single ID for businesses; a phased shift to online registration; and a simplified, computerized one-stop-shop mechanism linking relevant agencies. Following successful implementation of the Plan, business registration in Vietnam has been reduced to five days and the computerized national registry contains records of over 650,000 enterprises. UNIDO's support to the country is continuing. By 2013, the aim is to achieve full online registration within one to two days for all investors in Vietnam and to enable information service users to also access audited annual financial statements of registered shareholding companies.

UNIDO began in 1976 to establish an international network of ITPOs in several capital exporting countries (see Chapter 2). The objective of these offices is to stimulate investors in their host countries to seek investment opportunities in developing countries, assist them in finding business partners and support those partners in realizing joint ventures. Today there are 11 ITPOs located in both industrialized and developing countries reflecting the emerging patterns of FDI flows: Bahrain, Belgium, China (two), France, Italy, Japan, Mexico, Republic of Korea, United Kingdom and the Russian Federation (see Table 2.1 in Chapter 2).

The ITPOs work in tandem with UNIDO's technical assistance projects and draw on UNIDO tools to help identify investment opportunities. One of the first of such tools dates from 1972—the *Guidelines for Project Evaluation*—a manual on the preparation of industrial feasibility studies, which became a standard tool for the financial and economic appraisal of investment projects. Several other manuals and guidelines followed (see Box 4.4) and their success can be gauged not only from their widespread use by policymakers and prospective investors, but also from their adoption by many universities worldwide as teaching materials.

Box 4.5 **UNIDO's industrial investment appraisal tools**

The widely used *Guidelines for Project Evaluation* (1972), reprinted many times, was one of the few manuals on investment appraisal available at the time of publication. A *Guide to Practical Project Appraisal: Social Benefit-Cost Analysis in Developing Countries* and a *Manual for Evaluation of Industrial Projects* both appeared in 1986. In 1991 UNIDO produced a *Manual for Preparation of Industrial Feasibility Studies*, a guide to identifying investment opportunities and carrying out studies and analyses to determine their viability.[19]

From 1983, UNIDO developed its Computer Model for Feasibility Analysis and Reporting (COMFAR), which was its first interactive appraisal tool. In 1995 an online version was produced (COMFAR III), intended as a complement to the 1991 *Manual*, and it has been upgraded annually (the latest version is COMFAR 3.2).

When UNIDO first produced its manuals some 40 years ago, they were addressed to governments and state-owned enterprises. The developing world has moved on since, but these tools have proven useful in a largely privatized world of industrial investment. The resilience of COMFAR, in particular, is evident from the fact that, although it carries a license fee for all users, demand is as buoyant as ever. In the two-year period 2008–09 UNIDO sold 1,750 licenses, more than in any previous biennium. All but 3 percent were sold to users in developing countries, and the large majority of these were purchased without the use of external TA funding.

Today there are many online project appraisal tools available to enterprises and prospective investors, but COMFAR remains attractive particularly for financial analysis. As a recent evaluation says, "COMFAR is a tool that correctly calculates financial results, based on a certain input following standard financial practices, and the model has been continuously updated to make it applicable in different business contexts. The newest

> version gives the users a large range of possibilities and it does it in 19 different languages."[20] While there are certainly more sophisticated systems on the market, COMFAR is used to help in the preparation of projects in investor-friendly terms and in analyzing and understanding investment proposals. Its particular strength would seem to be as an aide to training and capacity-building in financial analysis, and it has been integrated into more than 200 of UNIDO's TA projects. As a tool it is still partial, however, as it does not provide comprehensive analysis of development impacts.

COMFAR is used to appraise the investment project proposals of local partners and to develop national capacities for investment project appraisal. This matching of identified and appraised investment project proposals from developing countries with potential business partners from developed and other developing countries hosting ITPOs has been a standard UNIDO activity for 30 years and formerly involved the organization of investment forums. Through these forums, a portfolio of investment projects (and the local enterprises proposing them) was showcased at a national event to which the participation of international investors was secured by the ITPOs. The forum model, where local and international partners are brought together and assisted in holding business-to-business meetings, has spawned many similar initiatives, and today there are many such events organized by both the public and private sectors. At one point UNIDO was seen as being the bridge between the capitalist and (then) socialist spheres. Before 1989 there were ITPOs in Czechoslovakia, where UNIDO convened the first ever investors' forum, and in Poland. An investors' forum was also organized in Vietnam in the early 1990s.

UNIDO's investment promotion program consists of four main TA components.

Investor surveys

In addition to individual country analyses, UNIDO conducts surveys of foreign and (increasingly) domestic investors. The surveys use a questionnaire design that has been developed with external advisors and seeks to capture information on the broader consequences of FDI inflows. From these surveys, forecasts can be made of expected investments, anticipated employment growth, projected skill gaps, capacity utilization rates, energy and water usage, as well as investor assessments of the performance of different FDI-related organizations.

Investment monitoring platform

The findings from the UNIDO surveys are consolidated on a web-based interactive "investment monitoring platform" to which all stakeholders are given access. As well as hosting the survey database, the platform also supports the work of national investment promotion agencies (IPAs) enabling them to provide better information to private-sector investors. The data will help identify different types of investors, their performance, their varying impact on the host economy, their perception of investment climate parameters and expectations of the services they can receive from local institutions. It provides policymakers with the capacity to design policies based on empirical evidence and allows IPAs to design strategies based on institutional consensus and the private-sector decision-makers to come up with more rational business decisions.

Institution building

UNIDO supports the strengthening of national institutional capacities for FDI promotion, and in particular IPAs, which are assisted in developing better promotion, facilitation and image-building capabilities, as well as after-care and other services to both foreign and domestic investors. IPAs cannot succeed in isolation, of course. Even the best-run will not help to attract FDI in countries suffering from problems of cumbersome official bureaucracy, inconsistent policies, complex tax and licensing arrangements, macro-economic instability, distorted labor markets, and other problems inimical to business. Thus, UNIDO's program is also addressed to the broader policy environment.

Partnership exchange

Another feature of UNIDO's assistance is its Subcontracting and Partnership Exchange Program (SPX), which is designed to help enterprises in developing countries to identify opportunities for supplying larger company clients. The aim is to develop the capacities of local SMEs to meet buyer needs and identify profitable business opportunities for them. The SPX centers are normally located in a private-sector institution (chamber of commerce or manufacturers' association) or in an IPA or enterprise development agency.

There are three aspects to the SPX mechanism. First, matchmaking: a team within each SPX center, supported by UNIDO, first works to link buyers to potential suppliers or sub-contractors. It develops profiles of local companies and then helps to link buyers with competitive suppliers. Second, benchmarking: the SPX centers use a benchmarking scheme to enable local companies to compare their operational performance with that of other companies of a similar size and type, in order to determine more clearly their competitive position, and how they stand in relation to international practices in their sector. Third, enterprise capacity-building: local enterprises are assisted in formulating business strategies, developing investment proposals, mobilizing finance and identifying technology partners.

In investment promotion UNIDO is especially active in Africa, and its regional program AfrIPANet provides the best practical example of its work (see Box 4.6).

Box 4.6 **AfrIPANet**

The program is built around the Africa Investment Promotion Agency Network (AfrIPANet), which UNIDO helped to establish in 2001. AfrIPANet now comprises IPAs from 38 countries as well the UNIDO ITPOs. The regional program deploys tools that assist countries in measuring the impact of investments, assessing the relative quality of different forms of inward investment flows and identifying the investor groups to target with the appropriate instruments. The program undertakes periodic surveys of foreign investors that are present in Africa. Three surveys were conducted in 2001, 2003 and 2005. The most recent survey in 2011 had 6,300 respondents (domestic as well as foreign investors). It will be fed into the investment monitoring platform and provide a rich source of information to guide IPA policy on investment promotion. By the end of 2010 four countries (Ghana, Nigeria, Tanzania and Uganda) had established dedicated SPX centers and more are expected to follow.

UNIDO's technical inputs to this program include the survey methodology and data analysis that will be used to assist national agencies in formulating their programs; the benchmarking methodology for the SPX centers established within each country; the design and establishment of the monitoring platform; and capacity-building for national institutions to exploit the information on the platform. The ITPOs are also being mobilized for this program and a manual has been prepared to assist in understanding and benefiting from international business alliances.t

Technology promotion

Technology is a critical ingredient of industrialization. The link has been amply demonstrated by the East and Southeast Asian countries, the successful industrial development of which has been associated with rapid rates of technology adoption and conscious processes of technology management. In the early stages of their development especially, technology transfer occurred through FDI from the industrialized countries

The world is still divided into technology leaders and technology followers. The former category comprises the industrialized countries, which are engaged in scientific research and technological innovation and which have hitherto produced the overwhelming proportion of the world's pool of technology. For most of the developing countries, however—the technology followers—it is the management of technology, and its interface with production, that is important. The challenge for technology-follower firms and countries is to use technology to enhance their competitive advantage in national and international markets. Managing technology means tapping existing technologies, efficiently absorbing them, undertaking creative imitations and adaptations, and thereafter, improving on these technologies for productivity enhancement.

UNIDO can assist countries to develop technology management systems, for which a critical mass of industrial enterprises with a capability to adopt, adapt and diffuse technologies that originated in the technologically advanced nations is a key element. In addition, there need to be links with research and development institutions, educational and scientific bodies, technical institutes and industrial and technology promotion agencies in the public and private sectors. National technology management systems are thus more than the sum of the capabilities of individual firms in a country. They include the knowledge and skills within related institutions, driven by learning processes, ways of doing business, incentive regimes, and policy mechanisms aimed at strengthening technology management efforts.

Beyond the national plane, UNIDO can also facilitate links with international centers of technology. An example is the International Center for Science and High Technology (ICS) in Trieste, where UNIDO is a partner with the Italian Government. The ICS aims to transfer scientific knowledge through advanced training, support scientific communities in developing countries and economies in transition, sponsor individual scientists and technologists in developing countries and provide expertise in science-based technologies. ICS organizes conferences and training events, and maintains direct contacts with governments, public and private institutions and associations in developing and transition-economy countries.

UNIDO also encourages countries to go upstream in technology development and look into the future, through its "foresight" program. The purpose is to identify technology trends, assess threats and opportunities and develop scenarios of technology use that can guide industrial planning. In Vietnam, for example, scenarios were developed to assist the country to plan its science and technology strategy up to 2020.

Conclusion

The activities described under this theme attest to a wide array of different types of intervention, broadly grouped under a theme of poverty reduction. To test the validity of this objective, UNIDO conducted an internal desk review in 2010 on *What has UNIDO done to reduce poverty?*[21] summarizing evaluations undertaken during the two previous years. The evaluations of 52 projects were examined, well over half of them partially or wholly within the areas discussed in this chapter. The methodology used was based on the 2001 Organisation for Economic Co-operation and Development (OECD)/Development Assistance Committee (DAC) five-fold definition of poverty (see Box 4.7), as well as the two cross-cutting themes of gender and environment. Seven separate criteria were therefore applied to determine the impact of UNIDO's activities on reductions in "multi-dimensional" poverty.

The study found that overall "UNIDO projects and programs do contribute to poverty reduction, or hold strong potential" to do so. Most often the direct intended contributions to poverty reduction were in the economic dimension, with increasing incomes and job-creation as the most tangible benefits. By giving attention to occupational safety and health, some UNIDO projects also contributed to the human dimension. To the extent that UNIDO projects influence public policies and give voice to consumers, they can be said to contribute to the political dimension. The socio-cultural dimension was served by some projects which successfully involved previously marginalized communities. On the protective dimension, results were mixed: some projects helped to reduce economic volatility, while others fostered dependence on sectors vulnerable to external shocks.

The gender impact was also mixed, indicating the need for more mainstreaming of equality in project design. Many UNIDO projects and programs address environmental concerns, designed to directly benefit the environment (see Chapter 6). However, projects should be designed so that a more precise determination of impact can be made.

The evaluation thus confirmed that UNIDO had succeeded in raising an awareness of the poverty-reducing impacts of its activities. However, with the emphasis that the UN development agencies are giving to the achievement of the MDGs, orientated towards human outcomes, UNIDO needs to bring more rigor into the design of its projects. At the planning stage, baselines should be established against which to measure progress. Projects should explicitly incorporate verifiable indicators of outcome and impact to determine the extent to which human development has moved above the baselines.

> **Box 4.7 UNIDO and OECD's five-dimensional definition of poverty**[22]
>
> In 2001 OECD defined five dimensions of poverty:
>
> - *Economic capabilities* mean the ability to earn an income, to consume and to have assets, which are all key to food security, material well-being and social status.
> - *Human capabilities* are based on health, education, nutrition, clean water and shelter. These are core elements of well-being as well as crucial means to improving livelihoods.
> - *Political capabilities* include human rights, a voice and some influence over public policies and political priorities.
> - *Socio-cultural capabilities* concern the ability to participate as a valued member of a community. They refer to social status, dignity and other cultural conditions for belonging to a society.
> - *Protective capabilities* enable people to withstand economic and external shocks. Thus, they are important for preventing poverty. Insecurity and vulnerability are crucial dimensions of poverty with strong links to all other dimensions.

Most of the "productive activities" under this theme were also loosely related to helping enterprises improve their competitive positions on a value-chain. However, many of the areas described are pursued in isolation from each other. Some projects are quite specific to a country and an industrial sector (such as the cluster projects). Others are region-wide (agri-business in Africa), still others are generic and inter-regional (creative industries). Ultimately, in development, the most important frame of reference is the individual country, and the sectors within it. Concerted efforts to assist individual enterprises in a sector, and thereby address poverty-reduction goals, will need to depend on more joined-up approaches to technical interventions. Integrated country programming in UNIDO (see Chapter 1) has been an attempt to tackle the need for greater coherence but has not yet been rigorously applied.

5 Penetrating global markets

- Quality standards for trade
- National quality infrastructure
- Aid for Trade
- Conclusion

UNIDO's *Trade Capacity Building Program* has a short-hand description inspired by the value-chain: compete, conform and connect. Trade capacity begins with removing supply constraints and raising the international competitiveness of enterprises. Products are brought into conformity with quality standards on the global market. Producers integrate with the international trading system by connecting to markets.

The last chapter dealt in some length with the supply side (compete). It described how nearly everything that UNIDO does with and for enterprises in developing countries is to render them, and their production, more competitive.

In order for these enterprises to become part of an international value-chain, concerns of quality and marketing become of critical importance (conform). These are the principal subjects of this chapter. In terms of the international value-chain depicted in Figure 4.1 (in Chapter 4), it takes a closer look at stages 6, 7 and 8: standards, product promotion and the global trade environment. UNIDO has a strong pedigree in promoting technical standards, an area of activity that is becoming rapidly more complex and multi-layered by the day. In addition to longer established food standards, there are other important international system standards such as quality management, environmental management, and social accountability. Since 1995, in addition to understanding and conforming with these many standards, countries that have joined the World Trade Organization (WTO), or are aspiring to do so, are required to meet their obligations under the sanitary and phyto-sanitary (SPS) measures and the technical barriers to trade (TBT) agreements. More recently, there has been a wave of new "private" standards, often dictated by consumer demands.

When it comes to "connecting" with international markets, UNIDO's activities are quite limited because other UN organizations are working in this area. However, as discussed in the previous chapter, its work in promoting foreign direct investment (FDI) and assisting domestic enterprises in developing countries to integrate with the global economy through linkages with foreign firms is relevant to international market access. This work was also discussed in the last chapter.

In terms of disbursements, UNIDO is already the largest UN source of technical cooperation for trade capacity building. Aid for Trade (AfT) offers UNIDO new opportunities to assist the export efforts of the South.

Quality standards for trade

Even if there are some serious remaining iniquities for low-income countries, trade tariff levels have fallen over the years, helped by successive global rounds of negotiations. However, market access opportunities are still hampered by the need for developing country enterprises to comply with ever-more complex trade standards.

From health to environment

Technical standards to safeguard health are nothing new. Even before they were traded, products had to comply with standards of consumer safety. Trade standards reflected those in domestic markets but the proliferation of national strictures necessitated international normalization. Negotiated as part of the Uruguay Round of trade negotiations, which concluded in 1995, the SPS agreement of the WTO allows countries to set their own health standards on products "subject to the requirement that these measures are not applied in a manner which would constitute a means of arbitrary or unjustifiable discrimination between members" and are not a disguised restriction on international trade.[1] Also under the WTO, the TBT Agreement tries to ensure that regulations, standards, testing and certification procedures do not create unnecessary obstacles.[2]

Over the last two decades, however, trade standards have become more multi-layered and complex. To basic health and hygiene standards have been added concerns of an environmental nature, pertaining to the nature of production processes. More recently, the social ramifications of production have come into the picture and there are now broader issues of sustainability, including water use and carbon emissions (see Figure 5.1).

90 Penetrating global markets

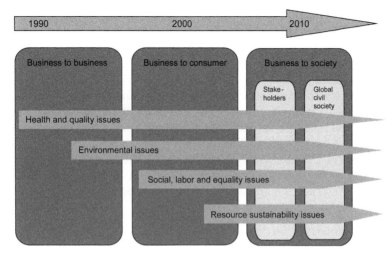

Figure 5.1 How trade standards have evolved
Source: UNIDO, Trade Standards Compliance Report 2010 (Vienna: UNIDO, 2011)

There are also the norms of the International Organization for Standardization (ISO), a non-governmental organization (NGO) custodian of a total of 15,000 standards. Its ISO 14000 series promotes sound environmental management; ISO 22000 concerns food safety; and the ISO 26000 series sets standards for corporate social responsibility. ISO standards are key, since many governments and private companies will only recognize certification entities the work of which itself conforms to them.

More private standards

Idealistic development movements (such as Fairtrade), inspired by consumer interests in the developed countries, have emerged to embrace the much broader concerns of asymmetric trade relations. They adhere to a range of basic guidelines of fairness both for producers and traders. However, while consumer conscience has given a fillip to poorer commodity producers in developing countries, it has added to the complexity of trading conditions, with a huge increase in the numbers of standards and labels attaching to exports. Apart from environmental and Fairtrade standards, which different products are expected to meet, there are increasingly sophisticated standards pertaining to the processes by which goods are produced and traded. Many of these are private standards, including those established by major retail organizations in the developed countries (see Box 5.1).

Box 5.1 Private standards and UNIDO

Concerns have increased in industrialized countries about food safety, chemicals, allergens and working conditions. Supermarket chains have been impelled by consumer awareness of quality, environmental sustainability, equitable development and worker-safety to push for exacting new standards. These retailer and civil society-driven "private" standards have emerged as new market requirements. According to some estimates, there are now more than 1,000, including codes of conduct and management systems. Enterprises in developing countries face the challenge of complying with the multitude of private standards, which incur costs, but which can also bring benefits in favoring specific niche markets.

UNIDO's 2010 guide—*Making Private Standards Work for You*—is focused on the footwear, garment and furniture sectors, and is intended to assist exporters and business support organizations in developing countries to better understand private standards and turn them to their advantage as they engage with global supply chains. Specifically, the guide:

- Draws on lessons learned from technical assistance projects;
- Gives an overview of the landscape of private standards;
- Provides an analysis of codes of conduct for buyers;
- Details the strategies that producers in developing countries can follow when faced with private standards, including the costs and benefits of compliance; and
- Includes a glossary of international standards and initiatives.

Thus, while some standards have been established for the express benefit of exporting communities and enterprises in developing countries, helping them to serve new niche markets, in the trade mainstream where large numbers of enterprises are competing to sell on the global mass market, multiplying standards can act as barriers. They need to be understood and complied with. They influence production processes, which may demand new skills and technologies.

Costs of non-compliance

In order to determine the potential losses from non-compliance with product standards, UNIDO has estimated the extent of border rejection for food products entering the US and European Union (EU) markets.[3] EU border rejections of imports from developing countries of fish and fish products, fruit and vegetables and products, nuts and seeds and products, and herbs and spices averaged US$72 million per year over the period 2004–08. Border rejections in the US market for the same products averaged $71 million for the same period.

These numbers are quite modest as a proportion of the total value of the same imports into these two markets. However, the compliance challenges for developing countries facing the regulatory requirements of industrialized markets are much larger than these figures indicate. Border rejections incite importers to avoid buying from a source country. In their turn the exporting enterprises from a developing country divert their products into other less exacting markets, losing them higher-value export earnings. The real potential losses for developing countries from non-compliance across the whole range of industrial goods exports are therefore considerable, and they provide part of the rationale for programs of technical assistance such as those provided by UNIDO.

National quality infrastructure (NQI)

Much of UNIDO's work in trade capacity-building is designed to help developing countries to meet product standards that global markets demand through improving their national quality infrastructure of standards, metrology, testing and quality. This architecture is concerned with conformity assessment, ensuring that quality standards are met, for which there need to be at least three key pillars: standard setting, measurement and calibration, and accreditation of conformity (see Figure 5.2). Developing countries require competence in all three areas.

National standards bodies (NSBs)

The first to be established among developing countries was in Brazil in 1940, and today there are standards bodies in the majority of countries. These standards bodies are responsible for establishing standards, both national and international. NSBs are normally members of the most important international standards organizations, including the ISO—which is effectively a federation of the (over 150) national standards bodies of the world—the International Electro-Technical Commission (IEC), responsible for some 5,000 international standards, and the International Telecommunication Union (ITU), a UN body which has developed some 4,500 international standards (known as "recommendations" in ITU jargon). These three organizations comprise the World

Penetrating global markets 93

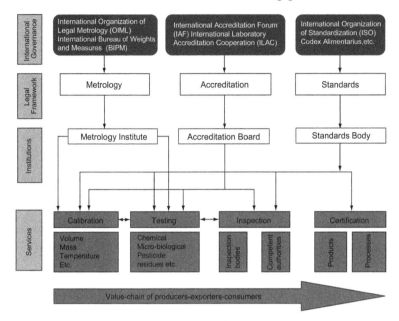

Figure 5.2 The architecture of national quality infrastructure
Source: UNIDO, *Meeting standards, winning markets* (Vienna: UNIDO, 2010)

Standards Cooperation (WSC). NSBs may also belong to regional standards bodies, which help to harmonize standards amongst neighboring countries. Regional standards bodies are particularly important where regional trade groupings (free trade areas) are established. The harmonization of standards is essential to facilitate trade.

NSBs in developing countries can take various forms, but, apart from the promulgation of national standards, their main functions are to represent the country in international bodies; contribute to the development of global and regional standards; raise awareness and inform national enterprises about standards; encourage compliance with WTO agreements; and undertake training in standardization. UNIDO has long experience in supporting NSBs in many countries.

In a recent example, UNIDO assisted in the creation of the National Standards and Quality Agency (Agence de Normes et de la Qualité— ANOR) in Cameroon. Following organizational advice, based on best-practice experience, ANOR now regroups under one roof the formerly dispersed responsibilities of standard-setting, quality and consumer protection. It is developing a national quality plan as part of the process of fostering a quality culture in the country involving the private-sector and consumer associations. Nepal was the first Least Developed

Country (LDC) to gain accession to the WTO in 2004. With accession came the responsibilities of compliance with the SPS and TBT agreements and UNIDO has helped the country to develop an institutional and legal framework for its NQI.

The East African Community (EAC), originally comprising three states, has now expanded to five (Burundi, Kenya, Rwanda, Tanzania, and Uganda) and a customs union established from 2010. To assist trade among the members, they are working to harmonize standards, and UNIDO has been helping them to create a common food safety framework, concentrating in particular on the newest members, Burundi and Rwanda. As well as helping to stimulate trade within the grouping, harmonizing standards will also help to increase trade with other regional African groupings.

National metrology institutes (NMIs)

Metrology is the science of measurement. Global markets—and indeed society at large—are reliant on the precise measurement of the mass, length, volume and other parameters of industry. The main roles of NMIs are: establishing and maintaining national measurement standards that are aligned to international norms; ensuring that there is a national calibration system usable by all manufacturing enterprises; and acting as the country representative in international metrology organizations, such as the International Bureau of Weights and Measures (BIPM), as well as relevant regional organizations.

Mozambique is one of the countries in which UNIDO has assisted in establishing a comprehensive metrology system which was lacking until recently. The country's expanding industrial base, and its growing trade relationship within the Southern Africa Development Community (SADC), has prompted the need to establish uniform measurement standards throughout the country. Through the Mozambican National Institute of Standardization and Quality (INNOQ), people are trained to teach officers in all the 43 municipalities to perform basic metrological verifications of measuring instruments and fuel pumps. Building on these foundations, a metrology system will be developed for more comprehensive industrial and scientific calibration.

Mozambique is a member of the continent-wide Intra-Africa Metrology System (AFRIMETS), supported by UNIDO, and established in order to help address some of the shortcomings of Africa's metrology infrastructure. With more than nine-tenths of African countries as members, AFRIMETS is a highly representative grouping which is helping to bring African measurement and calibration capacities up to a level at which countries can gain global recognition, while also facilitating trade within the region.

A mapping by AFRIMETS of the current status of scientific, industrial and legal metrology in Africa has revealed the gaps in measurement standards and legal metrology structures, leading to recommendations for the development of a regional metrology infrastructure.

National accreditation boards

National accreditation boards are a vital part of the conformity assessment infrastructure. NABs are responsible for accrediting laboratories, system certifiers and inspection bodies. Through an international peer evaluation process, a NAB can establish a Mutual Recognition Agreement (MRA) with the International Laboratory Accreditation Cooperation (ILAC) for laboratory certification and with the International Accreditation Forum (IAF) for system certification. Peer review ensures international recognition. ILAC was established in 1977 to promote good practice in assessment and certify international acceptance of the work of laboratories carrying out the work. IAF, established in 1993, was formed to certify quality management systems conforming to ISO 9001. Both ILAC and IAF have their own regional accreditation forums. In order to help de-mystify the complex processes involved in conformity assessment, UNIDO has teamed up with the ISO to produce a "toolbox," the key element of which is a comprehensive publication called *Building Trust*.[4] The publication outlines the basic concepts and techniques of conformity assessment and explains how accreditation works. UNIDO has undertaken a large number of technical assistance (TA) projects to establish or enhance the capacities of national accreditation bodies, which has involved helping them to reach the entry levels for MRAs and Multilateral Mutual Recognition Agreements (MLAs).

Mongolia was one example where UNIDO discovered that, not untypically, the tasks of accreditation were assigned to the single standards body, also responsible for metrology and laboratory testing. While a one-stop arrangement has its convenience, combining testing with accreditation raises doubts about an organization's credibility. Here, as elsewhere, UNIDO has recommended the separation of functions, helping to draft the necessary legislation.

In 2010 UNIDO undertook an evaluation of a large sample of its work in the area of NQI, encompassing projects in 17 countries with a total value of over $30 million.[5] A significant development finding was that UNIDO was generally able to respond quickly where a country's exports were facing a critical quality failure that precluded market entry. Helping countries to overcome quality gaps resulted in the immediate benefits of increased exports, a central rationale for SMTQ (standards, metrology, testing and quality) projects.

Many projects were concerned with specific aspects of the quality infrastructure outlined in Figure 5.2. In the same countries, these projects were sometimes complemented by those funded and implemented by other development partners. In terms of building sustainable capacity, the most impact was achieved when UNIDO played a more holistic role in quality strengthening and provided assistance over a longer period of time. Among development partners working in this area, UNIDO is well placed, as a neutral organization with strong in-house expertise as well as field representation, to play a central role in quality management. There are also key governance considerations, however. The evaluation recommends "multi-layered" governance structures in UNIDO's programs and the establishment of "national quality forums" comprising government, public and private SMTQ service providers, industry associations, and consumers in order to improve accountability and ensure that programs are demand-oriented. In any case, the greater involvement of the private sector, for whose principal benefit these programs are developed, is essential to any successful quality project.

In this area, as in others, UNIDO has encouraged horizontal skills transfer through South-South cooperation. In 2010 it established, in cooperation with the UNIDO Centre for South-South Industrial Cooperation (UCSSIC) in New Delhi (see Chapter 2), the South-South Training Facility for Testing Laboratories, in Hyderabad, India. The facility is based in the Vimta Labs, a modern business organization with a global reputation for testing and research. The center will help to train the staff and management of testing laboratories in developing countries, concentrating especially on food and agro-products. The training on offer covers a wide range of skills, including: analysis of contaminants, residues and adulteration, quality assurance, control measures, standards compliance, accreditation, and laboratory management.

Aid for Trade

The AfT initiative of the WTO provides the context and support for UNIDO's trade capacity-building activities. AfT had emanated from the Doha negotiations, in part as a response to the concerns of developing countries about the possible negative impact of some aspects of the Doha outcome. Today, with the receding prospects of a completed round, AfT has assumed even greater importance. Following the 2005 Hong Kong Ministerial Meeting of the WTO, a task force was created to set out a detailed course of action, with guidelines on funding, identifying recipients' priorities, needs assessment and monitoring.[6] The Task Force did not recommend a new agency to administer AfT, but stressed the need for a coordination mechanism, which the WTO secretariat has been providing. There is a large Advisory Group, whose members include UNIDO as well as the regional development banks, the Organisation for Economic Co-operation and Development (OECD), the UN Conference on Trade and Development (UNCTAD), the UN Development Programme (UNDP), the UN Economic Commission for Africa (UNECA), the International Trade Centre (ITC), and the World Bank. There are regular progress reviews, with the participation of all relevant stakeholders. These reviews have been held at two-year intervals, in 2007, 2009, and 2011. Successive AfT work programs are generated by WTO in order to keep the focus on trade assistance and give continued impetus to resource mobilization.

UNIDO has played an active part in the AfT initiative, which it sees as a platform to burnish its trade credentials. The initiative also encompasses the Enhanced Integrated Framework (EIF) for LDCs, also mooted at the Hong Kong Ministerial Conference and finally put in place in 2009. Its aim is capacity-building in trade for the LDCs, providing them with a stronger sense of ownership. The EIF secretariat is hosted by the WTO, and the eligible implementing agencies include UNIDO, which has developed several projects to be supported out of the multilateral fund of more than $200 million.

UNIDO also implements projects as part of another WTO-based facility: the Standards and Trade Development Facility (STDF). It was an initiative of the Food and Agriculture Organization (FAO), the World Organization for Animal Health (OIE), the World Bank, the World Health Organization (WHO) and, formed in 2002 and designed to assist in coordination and resource mobilization for assistance for SPS conformity projects, also helping to build alliances between standard-setting bodies and implementing and financing agencies. Membership now includes the governments of donors and developing countries, with observer status granted to organizations (including UNIDO) with SPS expertise. STDF does two things: through its projects it assists developing countries to enhance their expertise and capacity to analyze and implement SPS standards; and it acts as a vehicle for awareness-raising on the importance of SPS issues, helping to coordinate assistance, mobilize funds, and disseminate good practice in SPS-related technical assistance.

98 Penetrating global markets

In an exercise related to its AfT activities, UNIDO took on the task in 2008 of producing a "resource guide" in trade capacity building, on behalf of the UN development system. In 2010 it expanded its own brief and produced a second edition, which also covered the programs of 24 bilateral donors including the European Commission.[7] The objectives were at least three-fold. One was certainly family-mindedness. UNIDO under its current director-general has been keen to play up its role as a constructive member of the UN development system[8] and the first volume of the guide provides a substantial amount of information about the trade activities of 24 UN entities and of six other multilateral organizations (WTO and the regional development banks). A second objective—as the *Guide* itself proclaims in its Preface—has been to make the UN system more "strategic, focused and coherent" in the trade domain. Readers browsing through the two-volume compendium, however, will be either reassured about the extraordinary range of trade-related services available, or baffled by the richness of choice.

UNIDO will also have succeeded in its third objective: to confirm its own trade credentials by elaborating and comparing its range of activities in the domain. The organization is listed in six out of 11 trade-related categories.[9] This is more than most other UN agencies, although UNIDO's strength is undoubtedly confined mainly to the area of what the *Guide* describes as "compliance support infrastructure services," which have been described at length in this chapter.

Conclusion

The "conform" part of UNIDO's trade work is also the area in which it can play a more privileged role than most other entities. For one thing, product standards are a two-way portal. As globalization progresses and the exposure of developing country industries to global markets widens, higher product quality will result, first within exporting enterprises, but subsequently across other domestic firms. Trade is therefore the transmittal mechanism for a general upgrading of industries in the South, to which UNIDO is committed by mandate. Second, UNIDO grinds no axes. It is not itself a standard-setting organization for quality, and it brings an objective and developmental approach to conformity. Third, its global reach affords it a valuable overview of the challenges faced by different countries and regions.

The real challenge for UNIDO is to move beyond its work of institutional strengthening. With a relatively small team, the organization has helped a number of standards, metrology and other national quality institutions to raise their levels of competence and improve their services to enterprises, but these services are of an *ex post* nature. As a UNIDO promotional publication declared, "quality is to manufacturing what water is to diving: you cannot add it later." UNIDO needs to integrate its quality work more closely with its programs of enterprise support so that considerations of quality are built into improved (and environmentally cleaner) industrial production processes.

6 Greening industry

- **Montreal Protocol**
- **Stockholm Convention**
- **Waste minimization**
- **Cleaner production**
- **Renewable energy in industry**
- **Rural electrification**
- **Bio-energy**
- **Conclusion**

UNIDO's involvement in the energy and environment domains was boosted by the needs of developing countries to achieve conformity with several global conventions governing harmful substances emitted by industrial processes. The Vienna Convention led to the Montreal Protocol on Substances that Deplete the Ozone Layer of 1987, which specified steep reductions leading to the complete elimination of ozone-depleting substances. The Stockholm Convention of 2001 on persistent organic pollutants (POPs) outlawed the production of several toxic substances.

This chapter reviews UNIDO's activities in helping developing countries to meet their international obligations under both the above conventions, but its efforts to help in the "greening" of industry today go much further. In addition to programs to reduce all harmful effluents resulting from industrial processes, UNIDO aims at fostering fundamental changes in both product design and technology in order to enhance resource sustainability. The campaign also involves more recycling and a shift to renewable sources of energy. UNIDO leads the UN's advisory group on energy and climate change which has called for the adoption of a target to achieve universal access to modern energy services by 2030. The group has recommended launching a major global campaign of public-private cooperation to promote the use of renewable energy.

Montreal Protocol

In the early 1970s three scientists[1] in the United States hypothesized that organic halogen compounds, known as chlorofluorocarbons (CFCs), might cause the destruction of the protective layer of ozone in the stratosphere. CFCs were compounds invented in the 1930s and used mainly in refrigeration and cooling systems, and in many types of aerosol. Almost all CFCs and other ozone-depleting substances (ODSs) ever produced had drifted into the upper atmosphere. When broken down by ultraviolet radiation from the sun, these compounds caused ozone depletion, exposing humans and animals to skin cancers and threatening crop production.

Some of the initial skepticism, particularly from CFC manufacturers, was overcome by tests which showed that ozone destruction was attributed to CFCs, and several developed countries, including the United States, banned the use of CFCs in aerosol cans in 1976. Ozone became an issue of global concern the following decade and in 1985—the year when holes in the ozone layer above the North and South Poles began to be detected—20 countries signed the Vienna Convention, establishing a framework for negotiating control of ODSs. In 1987 over 40 countries signed the Montreal Protocol to that convention, committing them to reducing the production of ODSs by 50 percent by 1999. The treaty entered into force in 1989, and the following year in London it was agreed to establish a multilateral fund (MLF) to support the phase-out of ODS production and use in developing countries, by funding the additional ("incremental") costs incurred in converting to non-ODS technologies. A secretariat to oversee implementation of the protocol and administer the MLF was established in Montreal, becoming operational at the beginning of 1992.[2]

Box 6.1 **Ozone-depleting substances**

The most widely used ODSs are chlorofluorocarbons (CFCs), which have applications in refrigeration, air conditioning, solvents, sterilants, aerosols, and foam-blowing agents. Hydrochlorofluorocarbons (HCFCs) are transitional substances which have been used to replace CFCs in some of these applications, including refrigeration, air conditioning and foam-blowing, but HCFCs are also scheduled to be completely phased out. Other ODSs include carbon tetrachloride, used in electronics and chemical industries, methyl chloroform, a solvent, halons and hydrobromofluorocarbons (HBFCs) used in fire-fighting chemicals, and methyl bromide, used in fertilizers. The

102 Greening industry

> scope of the original Montreal Protocol has been steadily expanded to include a total of 96 ODSs.
> UNIDO, UNEP, UNDP, World Bank, *The Montreal Protocol: Partnerships Changing the World* (2005)

The Montreal Protocol was a triumph of multilateralism, described by a former UN Secretary-General, Kofi Annan, as "perhaps the single most successful international agreement to date." There were several reasons for the success, including universal recognition of an impending environmental crisis of global proportions, incontrovertibly verified by science; and the discovery of cost-effective alternatives to ODSs, at a time when the patents on some key CFCs were expiring. While private enterprise had sufficient commercial incentives to phase out ODSs, however, success depended on ensuring compliance. Developed (Article 2) countries and developing (Article 5) countries are held to separate timetables for phasing out the production and consumption of ODSs. By 2010 all ODS production and consumption were supposed to have been phased out in developed countries, with the exception of HCFCs. For developing countries, the timetable has been 10–20 years longer, but by 2010 only the limits on methyl chloroform, methyl bromide and HCFCs were outstanding (see Table 6.1).

Developing countries are assisted in the task of phase-out by four implementing agencies—UNIDO, the World Bank, the UN Development

Table 6.1 Montreal Protocol: phase-out of ozone-depleting substances

ODS	Phase out limit (end of year)	
	Developed countries	Developing countries
Chlorofluorocarbons (CFCs)	1995	2010
Halons	1993	2010
Other halogenated CFCs	1995	2010
Carbon tetrachloride	1995	2010
Methyl chloroform	1995	2015
Hydrochlorofluorocarbons (HCFCs)	35% by 2004 100% by 2020	35% by 2020 100% by 2040
Hydrobromofluorocarbons (HBFCs)	1995	1995
Methyl Bromide	2005	2015
Bromochloromethane (BCM)	2002	2002

Source: UNIDO, *Greening of Industry under the Montreal Protocol* (Vienna: UNIDO, 2009)

Programme (UNDP) and the UN Environment Programme (UNEP)—with the support of the MLF. Although the focus is on clearly measurable objectives of reducing ODS use, there are several aspects to the task in each country. These include awareness-raising (important for a problem that is highly technical, essentially invisible and very long-term), development of plans and strategies, strengthening of institutions and mechanisms to manage and monitor phase-out, support for enterprises in making technology conversions, and data collection. There is no strict demarcation of responsibilities among the four agencies, and there is an element of competition among them, which is not unhealthy. However UNEP, which instigated the international agreements and which has its own Ozone Secretariat, plays more of an "upstream" role in assisting countries with national plans to eliminate ODSs. A good example are the Refrigerant Management Plans, which cover the major proportion of ODS use in many low-volume consuming countries. UNEP has helped with their formulation and with putting in place the institutions and mechanisms for monitoring compliance. Although they also assist countries with sector plans, the other three agencies are more concerned than UNEP with the downstream investment components. UNEP also has a role in information dissemination through its clearing house, and through the network of National Ozone Units.

UNIDO began implementing its first Montreal Protocol (MP) projects in 1993 and its share of allocations from the MLF has grown to about 25 percent. During the 1990s the MLF grew to become by far the most important source of non-core funding, of which it accounted for 40 percent by the end of the decade. By 2010 its share had fallen to 14 percent (see Table 2.2 in Chapter 2), although in some countries MLF projects still account for the major part of UNIDO's activity.[3] To date, UNIDO has implemented over 1,200 projects in 85 countries, helping to phase out more than 70,000 tons of ozone-depleting "potential" (a normalized measure used to aggregate the totality of emissions), which is a little over one-quarter of the total.

The focus of UNIDO's work has been on six applications, where it has specific expertise: refrigeration, plastic foams, halons, solvents, fumigants and aerosols. A total of 1,250 individual enterprises have been assisted and many local institutions have been supported. There have been much wider benefits than helping to save the ozone layer. For example, in refrigeration UNIDO has helped to train many workers in the servicing and maintenance of equipment. In projects to phase methyl bromide (a pesticide) out of agriculture, thousands of farmers have been assisted to adopt more environmentally compatible alternatives which have increased their export competitiveness in the tobacco, cut-flower and horticultural sectors.

The ultimate elimination of HCFCs is the final major challenge under the Montreal Protocol. In 2013 a capping of consumption at 2009–10 levels is to come into effect and all countries will need to develop plans for phasing out HCFCs. In 2009 UNIDO was the first of the MLF implementing agencies to assist in the development of country plans. Macedonia and Croatia were approved in 2010, and plans for a further 30 countries were completed in 2011.

UNIDO's success in helping countries to meet their obligations under the Montreal Protocol—backed by generous MLF support—can be conveniently measured through reductions in potential ozone depletion.[4] The campaign has been something of a model for UNIDO, ideally suited to its mandate. A recent evaluation was very positive about the results, although it found that more cooperation with other UNIDO projects would have resulted in a more comprehensive learning process and more holistic approaches to the promotion of environmentally sensitive industrial processes.[5] UNIDO's Montreal Protocol projects have nevertheless had beneficial consequences beyond the reduction of ODS emissions. In replacing chillers, for example, improved technologies result in more energy-efficient processes which reduce carbon dioxide emissions, thus helping to realize the goals of the Kyoto Protocol (on carbon emissions).

Stockholm Convention

The Stockholm Convention on "persistent organic pollutants" (POPs) is an international treaty designed to curb and bring to an end the production and use of the world's most poisonous chemicals.[6] It was signed in 2001, after protracted negotiations managed by UNEP, and it became operational following ratification by the 50th signatory in 2004, at which time it had been signed by over 150 countries. Initially, the convention targeted the "dirty dozen" toxic chemicals.[7] Most of them have been used as pesticides or fungicides, but they also include chemicals used in, or by-products of, industrial processes. Despite widespread use in some cases,[8] they have subsequently been found to be hazardous to human health and the environment, where they resist degradation for long periods (hence "persistent") and can be "transported, through air, water and migratory species, across international boundaries and deposited far from their place of release, where they accumulate in terrestrial and aquatic ecosystems."[9] In 2009 nine additional chemicals were added by the Conference of the Parties to the list of banned or restricted substances under the convention.

Countries that have signed the Stockholm Convention (173 in 2011) are required to develop national implementation plans (NIPs) outlining how they will comply with the terms of the treaty, which specify the phase-out of the production and use of certain chemicals, but allow the use of others for specific purposes (for example, combating the spread of malaria with DDT). The action plans should determine how much of each of the targeted chemicals is released in the country, and how national laws and regulations will need to be modified to ensure compliance. As with other environmental conventions, there are regular "conferences of the parties" to review progress and agree amendments.

The Stockholm Convention is perhaps best understood as having five essential aims:

- Eliminating dangerous POPs, starting with the 12 worst;
- Supporting the transition to safer alternatives;
- Targeting additional POPs for action;
- Cleaning up old stockpiles and equipment containing POPs; and
- Fostering international cooperation to eliminate POPs.

The Global Environmental Facility (GEF) is the designated financial mechanism for the Stockholm Convention and supports UNIDO, as well as other organizations within and outside the UN system, in the implementation of projects to combat POPs. UNIDO supports all of the above aims of the convention. It has helped more than 50 countries to develop NIPs and is well placed to advise on the use of industrial processes and technologies which do not use POPs and which avoid their unintended production.

Waste minimization

An international conference in Dubai in 2006 agreed to the Strategic Approach to International Chemicals Management (SAICM), a policy framework and a basis for international cooperation. There is a secretariat hosted by UNEP and UNIDO is supporting projects in Africa, the Arab region and Latin America to help countries to devise chemical management plans.

For example, in Uruguay the objective of UNIDO's work is to help decrease the environmental and health risks associated with products using mercury, a valuable but dangerous substance widely used in artisanal gold-mining. With the recent appreciation of the gold price, there has been a substantial increase in mercury utilization worldwide. Small-scale mining results in the emission of some 1,000 tons of anthropogenic mercury per year, about one-third of the world's total. UNIDO is co-leader of a global mercury partnership for artisanal gold-mining, designed to halve the use of mercury in mining by 2017.

Since 2005, a new focus of UNIDO's work in chemicals management and waste minimization has been based on the concept of "chemical leasing" (ChL), developed in cooperation with a group of international experts.[10] Traditionally, chemicals are sold to customers who become owners of the substances and therefore responsible for their use and disposal. Their suppliers have a clear economic interest in increasing the amount of chemicals sold, which is usually related to negative releases to the environment. The ChL approach is much more service-oriented. In this business model the customer pays for the benefits obtained from the chemical, not for the substance itself. Consequently the economic success of the supplier is no longer linked with product turnover. The chemical consumption becomes a cost rather than a revenue factor for the chemical's supplier, who will try to optimize the use of the chemical and improve the conditions for recycling in order to reduce the amount consumed, which again reduces environmental pollution. ChL is thus a key element of sustainable chemicals management systems.

UNIDO has been promoting this approach globally, introducing it in eight countries in cooperation with the respective National Cleaner Production Centers (see below). UNIDO has developed a specific ChL toolkit to encourage a more systematic approach to the implementation of ChL at enterprise level and launched a global award for ChL in 2010.

UNIDO also has programs in waste-water management, introducing countries to technologies that improve water utilization and prevent the discharge of industrial effluents into international waters. One of the largest programs in which UNIDO is involved, together with other UN and non-UN agencies, is in the "Guinea Current Large Marine Ecosystem" (GCLME), a coastal region in West Africa where the industrial activities of 16 countries have had a deleterious impact on coastal ecosystems, affecting marine life and depleting fisheries. The strategic action program approved by the governments will lead to the establishment of demonstration projects and build capacity to manage industrial and other human activities in ways that will not harm the marine environment. Another GEF-funded "offshore" program is part of a larger Mediterranean action plan to preserve the marine ecosystem. UNIDO is working with institutions in Egypt, Morocco and Tunisia to encourage the transfer of environmentally sustainable technologies (TEST) to enterprises and bring about a reduction in potentially harmful effluents.

Another chronic and rapidly growing contemporary problem arises from the discarding of electrical and electronic products: e-waste. Since consumers replace electronic equipment at regular intervals, e-waste is accumulating rapidly: globally at the rate of some 40 million tons per year. E-waste contains over 1,000 different substances, rendering the problems of recovery and processing very complex. Most developing countries lack the expertise to handle e-waste effectively, especially as much of it ends up in the informal sector. Environmental regulations have not kept pace with the rapidly advancing sophistication of the electronics industry. To help address the problem, UNIDO is partnering with other UN and non-UN organizations with a framework called StEP (Solving the E-waste Problem). UNIDO's focus is on Africa where it helps countries to develop a competitive strategy for e-waste management.

Cleaner production

Sustainability in production systems is fundamental to responsible environmental management. As populations expand and development proceeds, it becomes ever-more urgent to discover ways to produce that are least harmful to the environment, both in terms of materials used and expended.

The term "cleaner production" has a strong pedigree. It was first coined by UNEP in 1990 (at a conference in the United Kingdom), endorsed by the United Nations Conference on Environment and Development (Rio Summit) in 1992 in its Agenda 21 outcome document, and formally defined in 1994 as "the continuous application of an integrated environmental strategy to processes, products and services to increase efficiency and reduce risks to humans and the environment."[11] In manufacturing and industry, UNIDO could easily perceive that it had a key role to play in promoting sustainable development.

UNIDO and UNEP began a close collaboration on cleaner production (CP) in 1993, when they worked together on projects in China and India. Their pilot projects in those countries successfully demonstrated the potentially beneficial consequences of CP in individual enterprises and suggested the need to create institutional arrangements to consolidate and replicate the experience. The following year, UNIDO and UNEP commenced their National Cleaner Production Centres (NCPC) program, the purpose of which would be to establish or adapt national institutions to provide a range of services (see Box 6.2). The first eight NCPCs had been established by 1995 and the program has since spread to 47 countries: 15 in Eastern Europe, 12 in Latin America, 11 in Africa, seven in Asia, and two in Arab states.

The NCPCs are professional centers that deliver the following five core functions:[12]

- *Technical assistance and in-plant assessments*: they work with individual enterprises to identify, evaluate and implement appropriate

CP systems. The models of successful CP applications created demonstrate tangible economic and environmental benefits. In some cases, the assessments target specific environmental or resource use concerns, such as energy efficiency or chemicals management. In other cases, a link is established with broader environmental goals, such as management systems or product development. Assessments are combined with training of staff to ensure sustainability and foster continuous improvement in resource productivity and environmental performance of the participating enterprises.

- *Training*: they train a cadre of national experts who can assist enterprises and other organizations in the implementation of CP solutions. For this purpose, UNIDO has developed a "CP Toolkit" and CP Award for experts and trainers.
- *Information dissemination and awareness creation*: they disseminate information on CP concepts, methods and benefits to raise awareness and commitment for CP. This involves the creation of websites and the publication of case studies, fact sheets and manuals, and the organization of seminars and workshops, often in collaboration with industry and/or professional associations. Individual NCPCs produce their own manuals. The Centre in Sri Lanka, for example, has produced a "how-to" guide for small and medium-sized enterprises (SMEs), as well as a best-practice awards scheme.
- *Policy advice*: they work with government agencies and other stakeholders in the country to create a conducive policy environment for CP. This may include developing new strategies aimed to promote CP or providing input for other relevant policy developments and strategies.
- *CP Technology and Investment Promotion*: they support the transfer of, and investment in, environmentally sound technologies (ESTs). Specific activities include: benchmarking and technology gap assessments; technology identification, screening and assessment; and preparation of investment proposals and business plans. In some countries—for example Colombia and Vietnam—technology promotion has been combined with the provision of "green" credit lines.

Box 6.2 National Cleaner Production Centres in four regions

China

The Chinese NCPC was one of the first to be established, in 1994. Affiliated with the Chinese Research Academy of Environmental Sciences, the Centre comes under the authority of the Ministry for Environmental

Protection (MEP) and is designed to provide policy and technical support to the government, although it operates with relative autonomy. The CNCPC numbers 26 staff and has an annual budget of about US$1 million. It is mainly active in the chemicals and metallurgy industries, brewing, building materials, fertilizer, and textiles. Although established with the financial and technical support of UNIDO and UNEP (with no separate donor funding), the CNCPC has been financially self-sufficient for the last 10 years, earning an income from the services it provides to manufacturing enterprises. The Centre performs at least three roles: (i) it provides policy advice on cleaner production to the MEP and other government entities, helping to raise awareness on a national scale about the importance of enhancing environmental efficiency; (ii) it is a training institution for enterprise managers, consulting firms and public officials; between 2001 and 2009 some 18,000 people received training certificates from the Centre as CP auditors, and (iii) it undertakes CP audits for enterprises, which is compulsory under Chinese law, and advises on CP options.

South Africa

The NCPC-SA was formally opened during the 2002 World Summit on Sustainable Development in Johannesburg. It is hosted by the Council for Scientific and Industrial Research (CSIR), under the auspices of the government's Department of Trade and Industry (DTI), which supports it financially. The Centre's annual budget is around $2 million and it employs 13 staff. It operates mainly in the following sectors: chemicals, agro-processing, automotive and transport equipment, metals and allied processes, pulp and paper, clothing and textiles, leather and footwear, tourism and hospitality, and commercial buildings. NCPC-SA has the following objectives: (i) to increase awareness throughout the country of CP among the industrial workforce, management, government, service providers and students; (ii) to undertake CP audits in enterprises across a wide range of industrial sectors; by 2010, 150 companies had received CP assessments and awareness training, (iii) to assist enterprises to realize greater value-added through investments in cleaner technologies; and (iv) to contribute to national priorities for energy saving, improved water quality and waste minimization. Among the achievements of the NCPC-SA have been the establishment of 25 waste minimization "clubs" involving more than 270 companies and a design competition to raise environmental awareness among fashion and textile design students.

Guatemala

The Centre (known as CGP+L) was opened in 1999 and is constituted as an independent, non-profit technical foundation, hosted by the Guatemalan Chamber of Industry. It has sought to improve its work by implementing the ISO 9001 and ISO 14001 international quality standards. CGP+L is small but active. With seven staff and an annual budget of $130,000 it has provided technical assistance in cleaner production techniques to more than 100 enterprises from different industrial sectors involved in tanning, dairy, metal processing, food and beverages, plastics, coffee, textiles and tourism. Other achievements include the preparation of guides and manuals on best practice in CP and the organization of many training and awareness-raising events. The Centre has developed an active collaboration with the government through the Natural Resources Ministry and has helped to develop a national policy on the adoption of cleaner production technologies. However, its independent status means that it also has the trust of the private sector.

Slovakia

The original Slovak NCPC was set up in 1994, but it has undergone various changes of status since then. From an independent civic association, it has become a collective of two entities: a non-profit organization with charitable status (PROVENTUS), and a private company, the SCPC, owned by its employees. PROVENTUS is responsible for awareness-raising and research activities, while SCPC provides professional consultancy services, remunerated training courses and technical advice, charging fees to its clients. Together, the two organizations have an annual budget that varies according to demand from $400,000 to $800,000, and a staff of between 10 and 20. The Centre has developed extensive experience in chemicals and pharmaceuticals, machinery, automotive manufacturing, pulp and paper, food processing, bio-fuel production, wood products, renewable energy, energy generation and distribution, and office management. It is active at all stages of the industrial life-cycle, from investment preparation and site selection, through construction, start-up, operation, modification, shut-down and decommissioning. The Slovak NCPC participates in European Union (EU)-wide cleaner production projects and has also assisted other countries with technical services, both within the region (Armenia, Croatia, Russia, Central Asian countries), and in Africa (Kenya).

UNIDO reviewed its NCPC program in a 2007–08 evaluation. It determined that cleaner production concerns are of critical and growing relevance in light of the need for more responsible stewardship of resources in an era of global warming. The program had been successful in creating many national CP institutions which had provided useful services to a clientele of enterprises, through awareness-raising, training and piloting; in some countries the NCPCs had had an impact on policy.[13] Box 6.3 gives three examples of enterprises that have realized significant commercial, as well as public gains.

Box 6.3 Examples of cleaner production in three enterprises

Kenya

Chandaria Industries produces paper and tissue products and, with the assistance of the NCPC in Kenya, implemented a program to increase waste-water recovery and recycling. It achieved a 25 percent reduction of waste and of waste water, leading to annual savings in excess of $600,000, with a very small investment.

Peru

Metalexacto is a small lead foundry. The implementation of several CP options, suggested by the NCPC in Peru, reduced the lead content in waste by 19 percent, enabled the recovery of nearly 350 tons of lead per year, and decreased water and energy consumption. Total greenhouse gas (GHG) emissions were reduced by 270 tons annually. Investment costs were low and recovered within several months.

Sri Lanka

Rathkerewwa Desiccated Coconut Mill, with the assistance of the NCPC in Sri Lanka, decreased waste output by 18 tons. It also achieved considerable reductions in water and energy use. Total GHG emissions were reduced by almost 1,000 tons annually. This resulted in annual savings of more than $315,000 from an investment of less than $17,000.

The program was in practice a collection of country projects which, while compatible with local conditions and institutions, lacked common program-wide objectives and provided little incentive for the creation of networks. With the conservation imperative growing, emphasizing the urgency of "doing more with less," UNIDO and UNEP have conceived a new phase of activity, which they are calling the Resource Efficient and Cleaner Production (RECP) program, designed to help enterprises in developing and transition-economy countries to achieve—through a process sometimes described as "decoupling" (see Box 6.4)—a triple bottom-line of productivity, environmental and social objectives.

RECP will strengthen the capacity of existing NCPCs and expand the network to new countries. Networking will include the sharing of knowledge among NCPCs and other RECP service providers, as a means of enhancing the understanding of RECP methods and assisting national institutions to achieve higher levels of competence in their delivery of services. Specific guidelines for NCPCs on good organization, management and governance practices to enhance the performance of the centers and other providers of RECP services have been developed. UNIDO and UNEP have launched a joint primer on enterprise-level indicators for resource productivity and pollution intensity. These indicators emphasize the links between resource use and pollution generation, enabling companies to monitor their use of energy, water and materials and their generation of waste and emissions.

The program features the promotion of "thematic" projects in enterprises and organizations designed to achieve commercial, environmental and social objectives. These projects are on themes such as low-carbon/climate resilience, sustainable tourism, e-waste, eco-industrial parks, sound chemicals management and chemical leasing. The program also helps to inculcate RECP principles into national policy frameworks, encourages financing for RECP in enterprises, and strengthens national innovation capacity for utilizing environmentally sound technologies and the development of sustainable products.

Like many well-intentioned development programs, RECP faces the huge challenge of scaling-up. Building on the NCPCs, the program has strengthened institutional capacity and produced many scattered benefits within enterprises across the 47 countries in which it is active. What is still needed is the development of national—and thence international—resource-efficiency movements encompassing private sector, government and civil society, in order to ensure that the benefits demonstrated at individual enterprise level are translated into successful industry-wide campaigns of economic and environmental betterment.

> **Box 6.4 Decoupling for sustainable economic growth**
>
> RECP addresses the need for decoupling of resource use and waste generation from industrial development and promoting the growth of productive sectors and entrepreneurship in developing and transition countries. Decoupling occurs when the growth-rate of a source of environmental stress is less than that of its economic driving force (e.g. gross domestic product—GDP). Decoupling can be relative or absolute. Absolute decoupling occurs when the environmental pressures are stable or decreasing while economic growth continues to increase. Relative decoupling occurs when environmental pressures are continuing, but at a lesser rate than the economic variable. Policymakers can use the decoupling concept to measure the effectiveness of resource and energy efficiency measures.

Renewable energy in industry

Globally, the industrial energy sector poses two huge challenges. In the first place, there is the challenge of climate change. Manufacturing industry uses one-third of global primary energy and contributes a similar proportion of energy-related carbon dioxide emissions. With a projected four-fold increase in the scale of global industry by 2050,[14] UNIDO estimates that industrial energy use is likely to grow annually at between 2 percent and 3 percent in the coming years.

Second, energy use is highly skewed in favor of rich and middle-income countries. Taken as a whole, developing and transition-economy countries account for 60 percent of global industrial energy use, and in some of them manufacturing uses up to 50 percent of primary energy. However, many other developing countries suffer from inadequate energy generation capacity, limited electrification, low power consumption, unreliable services and high energy costs. Recurrent power cuts, often unplanned, cause disruptions in economic activity, losses in production and can damage vital machinery and equipment. The impact of this chronic energy challenge falls heavily on the productive sector which is dominated by SMEs. In many countries, therefore, energy is fundamental to productive activities, particularly in rural areas, on which jobs and livelihoods depend.

Renewable energy can help respond to both these challenges. Climate change concerns, as well as the recent volatility of oil prices, have given new prominence to the search for non-carbon fuels and renewable energy sources. There is substantial scope for breaking the link between economic growth and environmental stress through increased energy efficiency and enhanced industrial competitiveness. UNIDO has set a goal of reducing primary energy use in industry by 40 percent by 2030. Together with improved carbon capture and storage, renewable energy can make a significant contribution to reducing GHG emissions. UNIDO projections suggest that, based on a medium projection of future energy use, 50 ExaJoules of energy per year could be accounted for by renewable sources by 2050. This would represent about one-fifth of total future energy use (see Table 6.2).

Renewable energy also holds considerable promise for meeting the needs of SMEs in developing countries, including—in fact, especially—in rural areas.

There are essentially three major sources of renewable energy for generating electric, heat and mechanical power. The capacity and suitability of the different sources depends on the end-use application. The most important source by far is biomass, followed by solar thermal and heat pumps. The industrial sector where the biggest single savings could be made is in petro-chemicals where biomass could partially replace naphtha and other carbon-based feedstock. Biomass is already widely used in some countries for industrial heat in food and tobacco, paper and pulp, and wood products. Bio-fuels, and their potential value to developing and transition-economy countries, are discussed in more detail below.

Table 6.2 Projections of renewable energy use in industry, 2050

Source	Favored industrial sectors	Use (ExaJoules/year)
Biomass	Chemicals, petrochemicals	9.0
	Pulp and paper	6.4
	Cement	5.0
	Wood	2.4
	Other	14.2
Solar thermal	Food, tobacco	5.6
Heat pumps	Food, tobacco	4.9
Total		47.6
Total global industry		230.0

Source: UNIDO, *Renewable energy in industrial applications: an assessment of the 2050 potential* (Vienna: UNIDO, 2009)

Solar power sources are not limited by resource availability and conservation concerns. Solar thermal energy has potential for process heating in food and tobacco, followed by machinery, mining, textiles and leather. Its application could be more widely spread geographically. Again, however, given the size of its manufacturing sector, China could account for almost one-third of the potential by 2050.

Heat pumps are the other major potential source for industrial heating. They take heat from the environment, or recycled industrial processes, without the need to burn additional fuel. Where the original heat in an industrial process was generated using fossil fuels, only part of the energy output of heat pumps can be regarded as renewable. The scope for the wider use of heat pumps according to UNIDO's 2050 projections is only 40 percent in developing and transition-economy countries, and the most promising sectors are food and tobacco.

Renewables are no panacea for energy efficiency in industry, and for rolling back carbon emissions. Economic factors can work against their wider use, and in particular the price of carbon-based fuels. The International Energy Agency (IEA) has estimated that a staggering $550 billion is spent globally every year on subsidies for fossil fuels, thus undermining the competitiveness of substitutes.

UNIDO has a role to highlight these distortions and their consequences for the use of energy in industry, as well as raising awareness of the possibilities for substitution. In its quest to "green industry" from within, UNIDO offers a range of services, including:

- *Technology demonstration*: promoting new methods and technological solutions in energy-intensive small and medium-sized manufacturing enterprises needing motive power and process heat.
- *Setting energy management standards*: encouraging the adoption of global norms, such as ISO 50001 of the International Organization for Standardization, which UNIDO has collaborated in developing.
- *Capacity-building*: strengthening the capacities of enterprises to manufacture, install and maintain renewable energy technologies and systems.
- *Policy support*: fostering agreements between industry on one hand, and national energy and environment regulators, utilities and financing agencies on the other.
- *"Global forum" activities*: convening entrepreneurs, institutions and decision-makers in policy meetings to raise awareness and promote international partnerships.
- *Information dissemination*: disseminating information on renewable energy sources and technologies and their applications; creating a clearing-house of practical applications; promoting networks.

Rural electrification

Worldwide, 1.5 billion people have no access to electricity, of whom 85 percent live in rural areas. However, access rates are very uneven and one of the starkest contrasts between different developing regions of the world—and a key measure of development progress—is the degree to which electrification has spread to rural areas. In East and Southeast Asia and in Latin America there is, with certain exceptions, a high degree of access of rural populations to electricity. According to the IEA, the rural electrification rate in China, Malaysia and Thailand was over 99 percent, and over 85 percent in East Asia as a whole. In Latin America the figure is 70 percent. In South Asia and sub-Saharan Africa, by contrast, the degree of access is markedly less, with rates of 48 percent and 12 percent, respectively.[15]

Access to electricity is fundamental for human development: for education and information, for the provision of health care, for entertainment, and for personal security. However, the provision of electricity through extensions of the national grid to rural areas is no guarantee of better livelihoods for the poor. Experience has shown that in unequal societies it is often the better-off households that benefit from electrification, since they can more easily afford the costs of connection and the appliances that are powered by electricity. Rural electrification is more likely to benefit larger numbers of the poor if it used collectively, and in particular if it is used to develop productive activities in which poorer households can be engaged and from which they can derive incomes. Also, extensions of the national grid may not be feasible in some countries because of cost. Local, off-grid electricity-generating solutions can be explored which depend on inexpensive renewable energy sources.

As part of its role as a leading UN organization in the field of energy—and particularly renewable energy—UNIDO has supported a number of projects designed to find local, sustainable and low-cost solutions to electrification in rural areas in developing countries, using small hydro-power, solar and wind energy.

Small hydro-power

Hydropower uses the potential energy of water by converting it into electricity, produced through run-of-river plants supplied by dedicated reservoirs. Micro and small hydropower (SHP) schemes have been talked about for many years as a response to the off-grid energy needs of remote communities in many countries with the appropriate topography. SHP can be used to satisfy low- to medium-voltage electrical needs for lighting and telecommunications, as well as motive power for small-scale manufacturing activities. UNIDO has been active in piloting a number of projects, mainly in Africa and Asia, using South-South cooperation as a means of replication.

One of the most successful projects has been in Rwanda, which has been a good example of South-South technology transfer, and typical of the kind of SHP that UNIDO wishes to promote. The project began with the contracting by UNIDO of a Sri Lankan consulting firm to construct a 75-kilowatt (KW) pilot plant and mini-grid. Following this successful pilot, the government then contracted the same company with its own funding to construct three additional plants of between 100KW and 200KW capacity. The first four SHP plants serve some 2,000 users, including small businesses, schools, health centers and households. Given the success of this project, and the commitment of the government to hydropower through its Ministry of Energy, the prospects are good for long-term sustainability.

Another example of an SHP project comes from the island of Nias, North Sumatra, Indonesia. Following the disastrous earthquake and tsunami of December 2004, UNIDO drew on relief assistance to support the construction of a small 40KW plant. Because of technical difficulties, the plant was not completed until 2008. However, it serves 200 households through a new community development center, supporting disaster warning, health care, education information and communication systems, and entertainment activities. UNIDO has supplemented the project with the provision of sewing machines, mills and other equipment to encourage local cottage industry.

While UNIDO has worked with more than a dozen countries to develop SHP pilot schemes, it also supports three international centers which are actively involved in promoting cooperation. Thus technical support (as well as equipment) for some of these projects has been given by the International Center for Small Hydropower in Hangzhou, China. UNIDO also has links to two regional centers, in Trivandrum, India and Abuja, Nigeria.

SHP is not without its complexities and these pilot projects have served to highlight the challenges involved. Before construction, the feasibility of each site needs to be carefully determined to ascertain the social, economic and environmental viability: who will benefit? What is the potential demand and will SHP pay for itself? Is the technology appropriate and well understood locally? What activities will be supported, since supply does not create its own demand? An evaluation of UNIDO's experience has advised that each project requires careful preparation to ensure that benefits outweigh the costs.[16]

Solar energy (photo-voltaics)

Solar energy is the largest energy resource available on earth and a variety of technologies exist for capturing it. These technologies include photo-voltaic cells (PV), concentrating solar power systems, solar thermal and solar water-heaters. These technologies use solar energy to provide electricity, heating and cooling for houses, businesses and industry. Given the variable nature of solar energy the electricity generated can be stored and used directly or fed into an electricity grid. Owing to ample sunshine in many parts of the world (particularly in the tropics and sub-tropics), PV systems are especially appropriate for dispersed, small-scale power needs, rather than for industrial applications, although in some developed countries the technology has been deployed on a much larger scale for power generation. With falling generating costs (of about 25 percent between 2007 and 2010), it is, with wind generators, the fastest-growing energy technology, with global production increasing at the rate of 20 percent per year. PV cells can be installed easily, conveniently integrated into existing structures (often as roof panels), and they have very low running and maintenance costs. Installations that are well protected and maintained can provide power for at least 20 years.

UNIDO has been assisting several countries to install solar PV and thermal systems for off-grid uses and industrial applications. The approach is to develop flexible reliable mini off-grid and on-grid systems for electricity generation, and solar thermal systems for productive uses and low-to-medium process heat for industrial applications. In Sierra Leone UNIDO has helped set up five "growth centers" in outlying regions, each of which is powered by solar panels. These centers offer business and information services to local communities, including lighting, computers, mobile telephone charging, food processing machines, televisions and refrigeration. Together, the growth centers cater to 150,000 youth visitors per year, with information-sharing on job opportunities, technology applications, commodity prices and weather conditions. The centers also have the potential to support entrepreneurial skills training. Similar projects have been started in other African countries. In Kenya, in a region characterized by small-scale farming, where households have no access to electricity and communications, UNIDO has helped to establish a multipurpose community tele-center as part of a larger rural IT project. The center is solar-powered and offers telephone services, internet access and a community cinema. UNIDO is also implementing a project to develop a solar-powered business information center in Mozambique.

As with hydropower, UNIDO has also supported the establishment of a technical center in China. The International Center for Promotion and Transfer of Solar Energy (ISEC) is designed to develop solar-energy technologies and encourage their adoption by developing countries. Apart from developing and upgrading solar energy technologies, the ISEC establishes standards for solar technologies, and helps to train institutions and staff of developing countries in the use of solar technologies and to establish pilot projects.

Wind energy

Wind energy has been harnessed for centuries to provide mechanical energy for productive activities such as grinding mills. For electricity generation, a wind turbine converts the kinetic energy of the wind into mechanical and then electrical energy. Because wind is a variable source of power, it needs some form of storage or back-up. The electricity generated can be stored in batteries and then used directly or fed into a large/ small electricity grid. Because of its variability, wind energy projects often involve hybrid systems involving other renewable energy technologies such as solar PV.

Installed capacity worldwide exceeds 200 gigawatts (GW), accounting for well over 1 percent of global electricity generating capacity. In some individual countries wind is already a major source. The largest capacity is in China, with 44GW installed, with 16GW added in 2010 alone. Next is the United States. India is the fifth largest with 13GW. Denmark has 4GW installed capacity, but has achieved the highest rate of wind dependence: one-fifth of total generating capacity.

Besides China and India, other developing countries have shown a growing interest in wind energy for household and industrial use. Wind-farms are still quite rare outside China, but there are already many small stand-alone wind projects with up to 5MW capacity. Among the countries with which UNIDO works is Cuba. The Isla de la Juventud, the country's second largest island, depends for most of its local power and heating needs on diesel-based sources. There are many barriers of a financial, institutional, technical, information and human resource-related nature which hamper the increased use of renewable energy sources. UNIDO (in cooperation with UNEP) is executing a project to promote the generation and delivery of renewable energy through the provision of technical assistance and financial services. The project aims to create the conditions for investment in wind power, as well as biomass gasification technology markets. The project has installed a wind farm of 1.5MW capacity to augment the supply of electricity to the island, and is setting up biomass gasifier installations at industrial sites for heat production and electricity generation. The project has also set up a "risk and replication management fund," designed to introduce innovative financial and institutional inducements for private investment in renewable energy.

UNIDO has also supported the Economic Commission of West African States (ECOWAS) in establishing the 15-country ECOWAS Centre for Renewable Energy and Energy Efficiency (ECREEE) in Praia, Cape Verde, the aim of which is to promote innovation and ensure greater energy security by drawing on the renewable resources of the member countries and creating a regional market. UNIDO and ECREEE are major partners in the large GEF-funded Strategic Programme on Energy in West Africa, which has a strong emphasis on renewable sources.

ECREEE and the Cuban project exemplify a more holistic approach to local energy needs, combining more than one renewable source. Having piloted a number of different renewable energy technologies, UNIDO is expecting to become increasingly engaged in helping countries to devise suitable energy policies for households, institutions and enterprises, drawing on a choice of suitable technologies. Beyond electrification using SHP, solar or wind sources, bio-energy also holds promise as an alternative energy source, substituting directly for hydro-carbons.

Bio-energy

Bio-energy is derived from any organic matter available on a renewable basis, including feedstocks from agro-processing residues, energy plants and crops, municipal solid wastes, human and animal wastes, and diverse organic matter. These feedstocks can be used in various technology applications to generate heat, electricity, and gas and liquid fuels. The range of technologies for bio-energy feedstock conversion depends on the final energy form required and the nature of the input feedstock. Conversion technology examples include direct combustion boilers, gasifiers, biogas systems, and bio-fuels (ethanol/methanol bio-diesel) systems. All forms of bio-energy can be used as direct substitutes for carbon-based fuels, and to the extent that they can be produced inexpensively using locally grown produce or waste materials, they are a valuable fuel substitute in developing countries that are heavily dependent on imported oil and gas.

Bio-fuels can be economically attractive, but while they substitute for hydro-carbons, their use is not always climate-friendly. For example, the burning of rice husks to produce heat for industrial processes will save methane emissions from otherwise discarded agricultural residues, but will add to the carbon load of the atmosphere. Bio-fuels have also courted controversy because of the competition for limited land resources of crops grown for ethanol with crops grown for food. During 2007–08, when food prices rose markedly worldwide, large-scale ethanol production from maize and sugar was blamed for shortages in the production of those crops.[17] There is no doubt that bio-fuel production was a contributory factor in the case of maize, and there have been concerns that wheat, palm oil, rapeseed, soy and other crops grown for bio-fuels will compete with food crops.[18] Hence the concern with finding sustainable ways to develop biomass for fuel. Bio-fuels can also be made from inedible plants. An example is jatropha, which is a native of South America but also grown in Asia and Africa. One of its main uses is for enclosure, since jatropha shrubs are fast-growing and dense, and not subject to animal browsing. The plant produces seeds containing oil which can be converted into bio-fuel. It has been used in India, Indonesia and other developing countries as a substitute for diesel fuel.[19]

As mentioned above, bio-fuels can be an attractive renewable alternative energy in industrial sectors, especially where they can be locally sourced. UNIDO estimates that more than 80 percent of the potential use of biomass for process heat in industry could be found in developing (and Eastern European) countries. The most promising are chemicals and petrochemicals, non-metallic minerals, paper and pulp, and wood and wood products, but not exclusively: in Brazil, for example, bio-fuels already account for 34 percent of energy consumption in cement manufacture and 40 percent in the iron and steel sector.

For developing and transition-economy countries seeking to increase their utilization of bio-energy, UNIDO undertakes research and piloting of bio-fuel solutions, provides policy advice to institutions and enterprises, and acts as a clearing house of information based on practical experience.

Bio-energy is currently source-dependent and countries have highly varied production potential. Ultimately, however, it will be global market conditions that determine the extent to which bio-fuels are developed and adopted. A key parameter is the price of petroleum products. Crude oil price increases add to the commercial viability of bio-fuels, but retail prices are heavily subsidized in many countries, artificially boosting demand. Another important condition is freer international trading conditions, which would help to make bio-fuels more accessible to countries that import most of their energy needs and have limited capacity for biomass production.

Hydrogen technology

Hydrogen is produced in substantial and growing quantities and is primarily used for fertilizer and in the petrochemical industry for hydrocracking. The possibility of using hydrogen as a power source has also been known since the nineteenth century, but while technically feasible, it is not yet economical for industrial, transportation and other applications on a large scale. However, concerns over climate change and higher costs of hydro-carbons have sustained the interest in hydrogen, which releases almost no pollutants or gases when used. It can be used for surface and air transportation, for heat production, and for the production of electricity, directly in the form of fuel cells or indirectly through gas and steam turbine-driven generators.

Hydrogen is known as an energy carrier and requires primary sources to manufacture it, but these sources can be renewable. From an industrial development perspective fuel cells are of particular interest since they can replace internal combustion engines and turbines to convert chemical energy into kinetic or electrical energy. UNIDO promotes the development and adoption of hydrogen technologies in developing countries and economies in transition. It has partnered with the Turkish Ministry of Energy and Natural Resources to found the International Centre for Hydrogen Energy Technologies (ICHET) in Istanbul in 2004. ICHET extends technical and financial support to hydrogen energy demonstration projects, undertakes research and provides training and education programs. It has helped to produce a number of prototype products, including hydrogen-fuelled rickshaws, buses and boats, as well as back-up energy systems. ICHET has developed joint projects and collaborative ventures with the Organization of Black Sea Cooperation, the European Commission, IEA, and other institutions in the public sector, as well as with private enterprises.

Conclusion

The success of the Montreal Protocol has demonstrated that international cooperation, backed by the necessary resources and consistent with commercial entrepreneurship to ensure compliance, can turn back a major climatic threat. UNIDO's mandate enables it to play a leading role in reducing the emission of ODSs. Montreal was also the spearhead of its current "greening industry" campaign, which is concerned both with mitigating the range of harmful emissions from industrial processes and with rendering those processes themselves more sustainable. Through its "greening industry" work, UNIDO can legitimately claim to be making a tangible contribution to the achievement of the UN's Millennium Development Goals (MDGs): both MDG 7 on ensuring environmental sustainability and MDG 8 on developing global partnerships.

The use of energy will be central to the greening of industry, and UNIDO's leadership of UN-Energy (grouping the UN organizations and agencies with energy interests) will ensure that energy remains a strong focus of its operations. UN-Energy in the coming years will support the Sustainable Energy for All Campaign (see Box 6.5). In September 2011 the director-general of UNIDO became the co-chair (with a private-sector representative) of a High-Level Group to lead the campaign.

UNIDO has thus raised its energy profile at a time when the world has begun to focus more intently on the search for alternatives to carbon fuels. However, it is entering a highly competitive field, which already contains many organizations with highly specialized technical expertise. In 2009, moreover, some European countries led by Germany decided to create the International Renewable Energy Agency (IRENA), not under UNIDO auspices, nor even within the UN system. The headquarters will be in Abu Dhabi,[20] although there will be a liaison office in Vienna. For UNIDO, the green industry context will be critical. It is specifically in industrial processes, rather than in more free-standing energy-generation initiatives, where its future lies.

Box 6.5 **Sustainable Energy for All campaign, 2012–30**

UN-Energy, a collaboration of 20 UN agencies and organizations, has declared 2012 as the International Year of Sustainable Energy for All, which will signal the start of a campaign designed to run until 2030. The campaign aims by 2030 to:

- Ensure universal access to modern energy services;
- Reduce global energy intensity by 40 percent; and
- Increase renewable energy use globally by 30 percent.

The campaign will focus on four principal areas:

- *Electrification*: to encourage the use of renewable and low-carbon technologies to provide convenient sources of energy through grid extensions, creation of mini-grids and off-grid household systems.

- *Clean cooking*: to help foster a thriving cooking stove industry, aiming at the adoption of clean and safe household cooking solutions for 100 million additional households.
- *Bio-energy*: to promote environmentally friendly biomass solutions to provide energy from the land.
- *Efficiency*: to improve the efficiency of electric power generation, transmission and end-use to reduce costs and expand availability.

UN Foundation, www.unfoundation.org; www.un.org/en/events/sustainableenergyforall

7 Facing the future

- Organizational rationale
- Future priorities
- Organizational effectiveness
- Connecting with clients
- Conclusion: staying relevant

Organizational rationale

The early history of UNIDO reveals that it came into being in a rather different manner from other UN organizations. One rationale for an industrial development organization would have been the need for standards to facilitate global cooperation through the harmonization of technical norms. The most obvious instances were in the field of communications (the International Telecommunication Union and Universal Postal Union, formed in the nineteenth century and absorbed into the UN system after the war), and international transportation (the International Maritime Organization and the International Civil Aviation Organization). When it came to industrial standards, a group of mostly American and British engineers got together and formed the International Organization for Standardization (ISO) in 1946. It was not "brought into relation" with the UN system, as the UN charter prescribed for specialized agencies, partly because it comprised many non-governmental interests from the beginning.[1] The ISO, however, is the nearest thing to an industrial standards organization, which explains why UNIDO does not itself set standards, but also why UNIDO finds itself collaborating very closely with it because quality standards are important to industrial development.

Other UN specialized agencies were established around international professional and scientific constituencies, impelled by the value of international exchange: the Food and Agriculture Organization (FAO),

International Atomic Energy Agency (IAEA), UN Educational, Scientific and Cultural Organization (UNESCO), World Health Organization (WHO) and World Meteorological Organization (WMO) are all examples (and WHO is also now best-known as a standards organization in the field of health).

Still other UN organizations were created in response to development concerns with necessarily global dimensions. The rationale for the UN Conference on Trade and Development (UNCTAD) was the inequitable global trading conditions and the chronic decline in terms of trade between the North and South. The UN Environment Programme (UNEP) came into being when it was recognized that the global dimensions of environmental stress demanded global solutions.

The UN was also called on to act as a conduit for the transfer of resources (including humanitarian) to developing countries. These funds are principally channeled through the UN Children's Fund (UNICEF), UN High Commissioner for Refugees (UNHCR), UN Development Programme (UNDP), World Food Programme (WFP), International Fund for Agricultural Development (IFAD) and UN Population Fund (UNFPA).

UNIDO did not tick these same boxes. Among the developed countries, which initially formed a majority of the UN membership, there was no other professional constituency of "industrialists" for an industrial development organization as such. Unlike UNCTAD and UNEP, industry does not have the same inevitable cross-border dimensions like trade and the environment that call for intergovernmental cooperation.

Yet, ironically, UNIDO has been the UN entity for which developing countries have clamored almost loudest from its earliest days. As discussed in the Introduction, development is a process that is almost synonymous with industrial growth. It was therefore natural that the governments of developing countries should look to the UN for advice and assistance in this crucial sector, just as they did for the development of agriculture and for the social sectors of health and education.

UNIDO duly emerged from within the UN secretariat but, in spite of strong developing-country support, there was a lukewarm reception from some of the industrialized countries. Ideology was a consideration. It was a time when the world had become polarized between East and West. The developed countries, which were the predominant voices during the formation of the UN system, and which have remained as hegemonic influences over its agencies, were ideologically opposed to public-sector sponsorship of the industrialization process, which was perceived as anti-capitalist.

During the 1970s, when the UN was riven by a fierce debate on the new international economic order, UNIDO was, with UNCTAD, seen as a standard bearer for the developing countries, which were then grouping themselves into the G77. The new international economic order (NIEO) was the origin of UNIDO's role as a global forum for negotiations, but while UNCTAD's agenda was formed around commodities, debt and aid, in which both North and South had stakes, industrial development was not an issue on which developing countries could exert the same leverage.

UNIDO has found its friends in the North, but a long-standing skepticism among some developed donors has never gone away. It is one reason for the absence of some countries from its membership today. It is also the reason for the imminent departure of the United Kingdom which, following the strong support that its government provided in recent years, has given very limited evidence of its dissatisfaction with UNIDO's work as a basis for its decision.

Future priorities

One of the obvious lessons of history is that UNIDO cannot win the larger ideological argument—however spurious it may seem to the proponents of industrial policy—and must continue to burnish its appeal as a partner of the developing countries by emphasizing the importance of those activities where free market forces are unhelpful to the industrialization process, and where a neutral public organization can add unique value. There are today three areas on which UNIDO can continue to build, and they all fall under the rubric of quality.

The first is the obvious one where—as UNIDO has often said—the most serious market distortions are occurring: the quality of industrial processes and the greening of industry. Although the figures are not exact, it is estimated that manufacturing uses one-third of the world's primary energy and produces about the same proportion of carbon emissions (see Chapter 6). The challenge of greening is therefore both urgent and crucially important. The Montreal Protocol was a natural entry point for UNIDO, which can take satisfaction from having helped to roll back ozone depletion through its interventions with manufacturing enterprises in developing and transition-economy countries, but the work of greening has barely begun, and UNIDO has the opportunity to greatly extend its work to assist enterprises to become less polluting and more energy efficient.

Green economics is firmly on the global development agenda, and the UN summit conference on sustainable development in 2012 (Rio+20) is intended to add impetus to the drive for environmental sustainability, alternative energy development and energy efficiency.

128 *Facing the future*

The UN often relies too much on exhortation rather than action, but if new environment accords are negotiated post-Kyoto which establish limits on carbon emissions, and a growing number of developing countries seek additional assistance in developing clean manufacturing, then UNIDO's services could be in demand. There is also a cross-over of the environment with international trade. Some of the most contentious issues in trade negotiations are environment-related, such as border tax adjustments on carbon-intensive exports, the role of intellectual property rights on climate-friendly technologies, and the likely emergence of new carbon-related standards, which could act as technical barriers to trade. In the two major ongoing domains of global negotiations, therefore, UNIDO could envisage growing opportunities for its assistance, applied to all three of UNIDO's principal constituencies: policymakers, institutions and enterprises

The second area is quality of products and systems. UNIDO is not a standard-setting but a "standard-getting" organization in the sense that it helps countries and their enterprises to understand the practical implications of quality standards and assists compliance. It has worked in the area of quality infrastructure for many years, and it is again trade opportunities that have heightened the importance of precision and quality in industrial production. UNIDO understands well the quality infrastructure that developing and transition-economy countries need in order to be able to compete effectively in domestic and international markets and it has established a long record of institutional strengthening. UNIDO has built an entire focus area—trade capacity-building—around quality standards. Helping developing countries to meet quality standards is the main source of its non-core assistance in this area, and it has enabled the organization to claim its position as the major UN player in trade-related technical assistance.

This second quality agenda, however, is bigger than "trade capacity-building" and should encompass competitiveness in a broader sense, being targeted at enterprises and supporting institutions. Whether for domestic or foreign markets, this area of priority needs to be concerned with quality along the whole chain of industrial production and not concentrating too heavily, as at present, on *ex post* quality concerns. In food production, there are concerns of health and safety "from farm to fork." In textiles and garments, quality starts with raw materials and moves through to design. In all industrial processes, product and systems quality is fundamental for the competitiveness of enterprises.

Third, there is "development quality," where assistance is targeted in particular at policymakers. While industry needs to be clean and competitive, UNIDO is concerned with the wider developmental impacts.

This book has highlighted the importance of industrialization as a motor of the development process, but the quality of development is determined by its inclusiveness, whether inclusion connotes gender, income group, rural/urban balance or (sub-national) region. Inclusion is the key to poverty-reduction in the industrialization process. Fostering productive activities among poorer, remote and marginalized people creates and sustains livelihoods by generating incomes and jobs.

History has been the witness to industrialization in its most brutish and debilitating forms, but, as this book has tried to illustrate, there are growing opportunities for even the poorest communities to engage in the transformation of food and raw materials, and become part of productive value-chains. As UNIDO's analysis of industrial policy reveals, however, only the right top-level choices will determine whether the paths to industrialization will be pro-poor. UNIDO needs to be the loudest public advocate of those choices, while in its operations it needs to build poverty-reduction objectives and indicators more explicitly into its projects.

Organizational effectiveness

Highlighting quality as the future priority for UNIDO is not to deny the importance of other areas in which the organization is active. However, none of them so readily meets the twin tests mentioned above: overcoming market distortions and the provision of unique services. Like all parts of the UN development system, UNIDO faces growing competition from other development organizations, but more especially from the private sector. The fact that it can offer advice and information free of charge, or less expensively, than other non-UN sources is not itself a reason for pursuing a particular area of activity, if those services are not the very best available. Focusing on what it does best, and for which it has the clearest rationale, will imply the need for some redeployment within the organization.

UNIDO has pulled itself back from its nadir in the mid-1990s. It continues to improve its working and reporting methods. The age profile of its staff suggests that there will be a continuing rapid renewal process at the senior level of the organization because of impending retirements. Renewal provides an opportunity to attract and promote the best talent in its most promising domains.

A narrowing of its focus is desirable for other reasons. Compared with 20 years ago, it is doing more with fewer people, but while it has reduced the number of its projects, in 2012 it will still be managing over 600 in more than 100 countries. One reason for this high number has been its readiness to take on non-core funding in several areas, even if it means a dilution of its priorities. A recent thematic evaluation stated that "increasing the sheer number and volume of technical assistance projects should not be UNIDO's top priority, but the organization should rigorously apply its own priority planning and quality criteria, which may mean occasionally 'saying no' to donors."[2]

UNIDO has achieved a consolidation of its structure, from five to zero deputy directors-general and from six divisions to three in the late 1990s. In 2011 further consolidation brought all technical cooperation and field services into a single division. There remains a large breadth of expertise, which can be a strength, but there is insufficient cross-organizational coherence and cooperation. UNIDO—like other UN organizations—could achieve greater impact through more holistic and multidisciplinary approaches. Integrated country programming (and "country service frameworks") began with much promise in 1998 and has gone some way toward consolidation. A 2010 evaluation found that the "opportunities for intra-programme and intra-UNIDO synergies were underexploited."[3] There is also a need to link the technical assistance functions of the organization with those of research and policy. In reaction, the organization has adopted the concept of "delivering as one UNIDO" (in its mission statement), and is configuring its new internal IT systems as a platform to promote more internal coherence.

Geographical consolidation should be another objective. For an organization of its present size, UNIDO spreads itself too thinly in its operations. UN organizations tend to plead universality in defense of their attempts to be active in as many countries as possible, but universality should apply mainly to the tools, information, research and other global public goods that the organization generates. Attempting to undertake projects in too many countries detracts from impact and sustainability. It would be better for UNIDO to concentrate on helping to transform industrial sectors in developing countries a few at a time, rather than making more numerous and limited interventions in many.

Connecting with clients

This book has written positively about UNIDO's cultivation of partnerships. Within the UN development family, where greater coherence is needed, UNIDO has been an example of collaboration under its present director-general—one reason why it has earned a coordination role in the field of energy. Outside the system, and with the private sector also, UNIDO has sought to forge productive links. If it is to concentrate on "greening" and quality, then it must seek to cement ever-closer partnerships with relevant organizations. In the case of industrial standards, UNIDO and ISO programs should be closely aligned.

Technical centers

For the future, the other important links are likely to be with developing countries themselves, but these and all partnerships need to be strategically managed. There are Investment and Technology Promotion Offices (ITPOs) in two developing countries: Bahrain and China. If their number is to be increased, the ITPOs could be transformed into full-fledged centers offering a range of industrial development services.

In some developing countries UNIDO has agreed to put its name to technical centers. This book has already mentioned some of the global and regional centers designed to promote South-South cooperation. There are now 10 UNIDO-associated "international technology centers" in developing countries, of which six are in China. The host countries of these centers see them as showcases for their own technologies and expertise (analogously with traditional bilateral aid), and with some of them, the connections with UNIDO's programs are quite tenuous. UNIDO should be more selective in determining the centers to which it puts its name, requiring that they are strongly aligned to the organization's own programs and that they act primarily as hubs for South-South exchange in a world in which the patterns of globalization are becoming increasingly horizontal.

Networks and networking

Networks are a more promising area of UNIDO involvement. The strongest are those that manage themselves and are self-generating, driven by the common interests of the membership. While the Resource Efficient and Cleaner Production (RECP) program, based on the 47-country National Cleaner Production Center (NCPC) network described in Chapter 6, is not yet an example of an independent network, the program is closely aligned to one of UNIDO's most important priority areas of concern, and it should be nurtured and expanded with continuing technical, and diminishing financial, support.

The RECP is the basis of an extensive knowledge network in cleaner production. In this and the other areas of its work, UNIDO can aspire to become a rich source of practical information and guidance, based on its experience of more than 50 years of industrial development promotion. Its research and statistics programs are of good quality, but they are far from unique. UNIDO's added value should be in demonstrating empirical solutions to the policy challenges of industrialization, derived directly from its own work and the experience of the many enterprises and institutions with which it is associated.

In 2011 UNIDO published *Networks for Prosperity: Achieving Development Goals through Knowledge-Sharing*. It recommended that:

> International organizations should improve their inter-institutional information and knowledge exchange systems and facilitate better knowledge networking among their members. This may include, inter alia, improving thematic information exchange in communities of practice, to provide more user-friendly platforms for knowledge sharing among members; to actively seek the involvement of non-state actors in consultation processes; and to actively support knowledge network development in relevant fields.[4]

UNIDO might do well to follow its own advice.

E-learning

Even when available in an accessible and user-friendly form, information and knowledge are of limited use without application. To transform knowledge into skills, UNIDO needs to change from being a relatively passive purveyor of information, into a more interactive learning organization. Traditional training events are no longer adequate, and they rarely guarantee the acquisition of new skills. UNIDO should embark on more full-fledged e-learning facilities, with benchmarking and certification to objectively record progress, test the capacity of the learner and certify it in an appropriate form.

Conclusion: staying relevant

At a time when the world is riven by financial, food and fuel crises, and facing steadily growing environmental challenges, UNIDO has to remain relevant if it is to be an active participant, rather than a witness, in determining solutions. It is not just what it does, but how it performs, which will determine its relevance.

In the summer of 2011, at the approach of a funding biennium with diminished core resources, the Industrial Development Board recognized the need for a renewed period of re-examination. It called for the establishment of an "informal working group on the future, including programmes and resources, of UNIDO."[5] The membership of the working group is voluntary and its timetable is open-ended. By the end of the year, it had held its first meetings and was receiving proposals from member states for its consideration.

Inter-governmental deliberations such as these have been important to UNIDO in the past, and the working group will help in determining the future direction of the organization. That direction must be primarily determined by the developing country members, the needs of which UNIDO seeks to meet. That might seem obvious, but UNIDO, like most of the rest of the UN development system, was a creation of the developed countries, which have remained the principal financial sponsors from the beginning. Over the years, more of this support has come with conditions determining the purpose and destination of the funding, as earmarked resources replace core funds. UNIDO still depends on a few large traditional donors, but it has begun to move away from its dependence on the industrialized countries and has succeeded in broadening the base of its financial support among developing countries, which have always been its principal source of legislative support.

Relevance is more likely to be assured when clients pay for the services they need. Thus the future that UNIDO can look forward to should depend more than ever on the developing countries, as active members and funders of the organization. This is as it should be, and arguably should always have been, in the UN development system.

Notes

Foreword

1 Jean-Philippe Thérien, "Beyond the North-South Divide: The Two Tales of World Poverty," in *The Global Governance Reader*, ed. Rorden Wilkinson (London: Routledge, 2005), 218–38.
2 Thomas G. Weiss, "Governance, good governance and global governance," in *The Global Governance Reader*, 68–88.
3 Nancy Birdsall and Francis Fukuyama, "The Post-Washington Consensus: Development After the Crisis," *Foreign Affairs* 90, no. 2 (2011): 45–53.
4 Katherine Marshall, *The World Bank* (London: Routledge, 2008); James Raymond Vreeland, *The International Monetary Fund* (2007); Bernard M. Hoekman and Petros C. Mavroidis, *The World Trade Organization* (2007); Ian Taylor and Karen Smith, *The UN Conference on Trade and Development* (2007); and Chris May, *The World Intellectual Property Organization* (2006).
5 Stephen Browne, *Aid and Influence: Do Donors Help or Hinder?* (London: Earthscan, 2006); *Beyond Aid: From Patronage to Partnership* (London: Ashgate, 1999); and *Foreign Aid in Practice* (London: Pinter, 1990).

Introduction: UNIDO and the role of industry in development

1 UNIDO is only one of many international organizations to be subject to the "hegemonic condition" of dominant donors. See, for example, Volker Rittberger and Bernhard Zangl, *International Organization: Polity, Politics and Policies* (Basingstoke, UK: Palgrave Macmillan, 2006).
2 Value added is the most common measure of manufacturing production. It is equal to net output after adding up all outputs and subtracting intermediate inputs.
3 Kaname Akamatsu, "A Historical Pattern of Economic Growth in Developing Countries," *Developing Economies* 1, no. 1 (1962): 3–25.
4 Shahid Yusuf and Kaoru Nabeshima, *Tiger Economies Under Threat* (Washington, DC: World Bank, 2010); John Page, "The East Asian Miracle: Four Lessons for Development Policy," *National Bureau for Economic Research Macroeconomics Annual 1994, Volume 9* (1994): 219–82.
5 A fourth country that is sometimes included in this group is the Philippines, but its economic performance has been much less consistent than the other three.

Notes 135

6 UNIDO, *Industrial Development Report 2009: Breaking In and Moving Up—New Industrial Challenges for the Bottom Billion and the Middle-Income Countries* (Vienna: UNIDO, 2009).
7 Rodrik, "Industrial Development: Some Stylized Facts and Policies," in *United Nations, Industrial Development for the 21st Century* (New York: UN, 2007).
8 UNIDO, *Industrial Development Report 2009*.
9 UNIDO, *Industrial Development Report 2009*.
10 Carlos A. Magariños, *Economic Development and UN Reform: Towards a Common Agenda for Action* (Vienna: UNIDO, 2005), 116.
11 Rodrik, "Industrial Development: Some Stylized Facts and Policy Directions."
12 Wilfried Lütkenhorst, "A Changing Climate for Industrial Policy," *Making It* No. 3 (2010): 16–19.
13 Ha-Joon Chang, "Towards a More Productive Debate," *Making It* No. 3 (2010): 23–29. The same author has also referred to the developed country position as "do as we say, not as we did."
14 UNIDO, "Industry in a Changing World," ID/CONF.S/2, ID/304 (New York: United Nations, 1983).
15 For example by Dani Rodrik: "Industrial Policy for the Twenty-First Century," paper prepared for UNIDO (Cambridge, Mass.: 2004), and "Normalizing Industrial Policy," Paper prepared for the Commission on Growth and Development (Cambridge, Mass.: 2007); and by Sanjaya Lall, "Reinventing Industrial Strategy: The Role of Government Policy in Building Institutional Competitiveness," G-24 Discussion Paper Series No. 28 (Geneva: UNCTAD, 2004).
16 See Stephen Browne and Sam Laird, *The International Trade Centre* (London: Routledge, 2011), which provides a description of the new trade theories of Paul Krugman and others.
17 UNIDO, "Industrial Policy and Private Sector Development," Internal policy paper (Vienna: November 2008), and "Industrial Policy for Prosperity," Internal policy paper (Vienna: UNIDO, 2011).
18 Nicholas Stern, "Climate Change a Market Failure," *The Guardian*, 29 November 2007, www.guardian.co.uk/environment/2007/nov/29/climatechange. carbonemissions.

1 Origins and history of UNIDO

1 See Yearbooks of the UN (New York: Columbia University Press, various years).
2 ECOSOC document E/2604, 19 May 1954.
3 UN Department of Economic and Social Affairs (DESA), document E/2670, December 1954.
4 UN DESA, document E/2670, December 1954, 97.
5 UN DESA, document E/2670, December 1954, 98.
6 UN General Assembly Resolution 2089 (XX), 20 December 1965
7 UN General Assembly Resolution 2152 (XXI), 17 November 1966.
8 UNDP was established in 1965 as a financing facility to support UN development system technical assistance. See Stephen Browne, *The United Nations Development Programme and System* (London: Routledge, 2011).
9 During the 1970s the Government of Austria constructed a dedicated Vienna International Centre (VIC) as a second European facility for the UN. UNIDO moved to its present home in the VIC in 1979.

136 *Notes*

10 Carlos A. Magariños, George Assaf, Sanjaya Lall, John D. Martinussen, Rubens Ricupero, and Francisco C. Sercovich, *Reforming the UN System: UNIDO's Need-driven Model* (The Hague: Kluwer Law International, 2001), 82.
11 General Assembly (GA) resolutions 3201 (S-VI) and 3202 (S-VI), 1 May 1974. Later in the year, the GA also adopted the Charter of Economic Rights and Duties of States.
12 Craig Murphy, *The Emergence of the NIEO Ideology* (Boulder, Col.: Westview Press, 1984), chapter 4.
13 All three institutions were nominally part of the UN system, but the governance structures of the World Bank and IMF gave weighted voting rights to their members, while the GATT's membership was fewer than 100 countries until the 1970s and its agenda was dominated by the interests of developed countries.
14 Second General Conference of UNIDO, document ID/B/155/Add.1, March 1975.
15 This was one of the few UN development targets that has been achieved on time. The share of developing countries (including transition-economy countries) in manufacturing value added in 2000 was 25.7 percent, although the major share was accounted for by China and the middle-income countries.
16 "UNIDO should be prepared to serve as a forum for negotiation of agreements in the field of industry between developed and developing countries and among developing countries themselves … " (Lima Declaration, para. 66).
17 Lima Declaration, paras. 26–27.
18 Ervin Laszlo, Robert Baker Jr, Elliot Eisenberg, and Venkata Raman, *The Objectives of the New International Economic Order* (New York: Pergamon Press, 1978).
19 Abd-El Rahman Khane, "UNIDO: The New Economic Order," in *United Nations Industrial Development Organization: 30 Years of Industrial Development 1966–1996* (London: International Systems and Communications, 1995), 56.
20 Magariños, Assaf, Lall, Martinussen, Ricupero, Sercovich, *Reforming the UN System*, 85.
21 Domingo L. Siazon, "UNIDO: Developing Private Industry 1985–93," in *United Nations Industrial Development Organization: 30 Years of Industrial Development 1966–1996* (London: International Systems and Communications, 1995), 67–68. In 1994 all five deputy DG posts were removed by UNIDO's board and never since restored, both as a financial savings measure and in order to avoid future competition for the post. At that time, there were nevertheless still eight managing directors.
22 See Craig Murphy, *The United Nations Development Programme: A Better Way?* (Cambridge University Press, 2006), 234–35; and Stephen Browne, *The United Nations Development Programme and System* (London: Routledge, 2011), 7–63.
23 COWIconsult, "A Future UNIDO" (Copenhagen: DANIDA, Ministry of Foreign Affairs, 1992).
24 COWIconsult, "A Future UNIDO," Preface by the Danish Permanent Representative.
25 The Commission on Global Governance, *Our Global Neighbourhood* (Oxford University Press, 1995), 282.

Notes 137

26 According to the constitution (article 6), withdrawal takes effect at the end of the year following the announcement of intention to withdraw, and contributions should be paid in full for the final year.
27 A rare exception might include the Generalized System of Preferences (GSP) in trade, negotiated by UNCTAD in the 1960s and 1970s. However, it has been argued that the way in which the GSP was implemented brought few long-term benefits to developing countries. See John Toye and Richard Toye, *The UN and Global Political Economy: Trade, Finance and Development*, UN Intellectual History Project (Bloomington: Indiana University Press, 2004). Also Ian Taylor and Karen Smith, *United Nations Conference on Trade and Development (UNCTAD)* (London: Routledge, 2007).
28 Ministry of Foreign Affairs/DANIDA, *Assessment of UNIDO: Capacity Development for Sustainable Industrial Development Under Changed Conditions* (Copenhagen, 1997). The team leader was John D. Martinussen, Professor of Development Economics and Political Science, Roskilde University, Denmark.
29 DANIDA, *Assessment of UNIDO: Capacity Development for Sustainable Industrial Development Under Changed Conditions*, ii.
30 Magariños, Assaf, Lall, Martinussen, Ricupero, Sercovich, *Reforming the UN System*, 102.
31 Magariños, Assaf, Lall, Martinussen, Ricupero, Sercovich, *Reforming the UN System*, 95.
32 *Renewing the United Nations: A Programme for Reform* (New York: UN, 14 July 1997), Document A/51/950.
33 See www.unido.org/index.php?id=1000965 for evaluation reports of integrated programs.
34 Ralf Bredel, *Long-Term Conflict Prevention and Industrial Development: the United Nations and its Specialized Agency UNIDO* (Leiden, Netherlands: Martinus Nijhoff, 2003), 135.
35 UNIDO Evaluation Group, *Thematic Evaluation: UNIDO Post-Crisis Projects* (Vienna, September 2010), www.unido.org/fileadmin/user_media/About_UNIDO/Evaluation/TORs/Post-crisis.PDF.
36 Kandeh Yumkella, "Towards Pro-Poor Sustainable Industrial Development: a Shared Vision for UNIDO" (Vienna: UNIDO, 2006).
37 UNIDO, *Annual Report 2010* (Vienna, 2011).
38 Department for International Development, *Multilateral Effectiveness Framework Report* (London: DfID, 2005).
39 Department for International Development, *Multilateral Aid Review* (London: DfID, 2011), www.dfid.gov.uk/About-DFID/Who-we-work-with/Multilateral-agencies/Multilateral-Aid-Review.

2 Current structure and mandate

1 The title of the position is deputy *to* the director-general, signifying that it is not at the level of assistant secretary-general, as for most UN agency deputies. In the reforms of the 1990s all the assistant secretary-general positions were eliminated as an economy measure and were never restored.
2 *Peer Review of the Evaluation Function of UNIDO* (Copenhagen: Ministry of Foreign Affairs of Denmark, 2010).
3 UNIDO, "Meta-Evaluation: UNIDO Integrated Programmes" (Vienna: UNIDO Evaluation Group, 2010).

138 *Notes*

4 UNIDO, "Meta-Evaluation: UNIDO Integrated Programmes," vi.
5 The "senior industrial development field adviser" (SIDFA) program began in 1967 with UNDP funding. By 1970, there were 20 SIDFAs in post.
6 See www.unido.org/fileadmin/user_media/About_UNIDO/Evaluation/Project_reports/E-book_ITPO%20Network.PDF.
7 The report of the High-Level Panel was published as *Delivering as One* (New York: UN, 2007), UN sales number E.07.1.8.
8 UNIDO, *Annual Report 2010: Partner for Prosperity* (Vienna: UNIDO, 2011), 3 and Appendix.
9 UNIDO website, www.unido.org/index.php?id=1000350.

3 Research and policy

1 UNIDO website, www.unido.org/index.php?id=7846.
2 www.unido.org/index.php?id=7846.
3 The work was led by Professor Sanjaya Lall, one of the authors of UNIDO's *Industrial Development Report 2002–03* (Vienna: 2002).
4 Craig N. Murphy, *The United Nations Development Programme: A Better Way?* (Cambridge University Press, 2006), 101.
5 UNIDO, "Industrial Policy and Private Sector Development," Internal policy paper (Vienna: November 2008).
6 For example, Dani Rodrik, *One Economics, Many Recipes: Globalization, Institutions, and Economic Growth* (Princeton: Princeton University Press, 2007); Dani Rodrik: "Industrial Policy for the Twenty-First Century," paper prepared for UNIDO (Cambridge, Mass., 2004), and "Normalizing Industrial Policy," paper prepared for the Commission on Growth and Development (Cambridge, Mass., 2007); Sanjaya Lall, "Reinventing Industrial Strategy: The Role of Government Policy in Building Institutional Competitiveness," G-24 Discussion Paper Series No. 28 (Geneva: UNCTAD, 2004); Ha-Joon Chang, "Hamlet without the Prince of Denmark: How development has disappeared from today's 'development' discourse," in *Towards New Developmentalism: Market as Means rather than Master*, ed. Shahrukh Rafi Khan and Jens Christiansen (London: Routledge, 2010).
7 UNIDO, "Industrial Policy for Prosperity" (Vienna: UNIDO, 2011).
8 UNIDO, "Industrial Policy and Private Sector Development," 3.
9 UNIDO, "Industrial Policy for Prosperity," 12–13.
10 Dani Rodrik, "The Return of Industrial Policy" (Project Syndicate, 2010), www.project-syndicate.org/commentary/rodrik42/English.

4 Poverty reduction through productive activities

1 www.undp.org/cpsd/indexF.html.
2 UNDP, *Creating Value for All: Strategies for Doing Business with the Poor* (New York: UNDP, 2008).
3 Small and medium-sized (and micro) enterprises account for 97 percent of businesses in developing countries, 75–80 percent of export earnings and 50 percent of total employment, according to the World Bank's International Finance Corporation (IFC).
4 www.ifc.org/ifcext/sme.nsf/AttachmentsByTitle/Background+Note+MSME+Data/$FILE/09278291.pdf

Notes 139

5 World Health Organization, *Equitable Access to Essential Medicines: A Framework for Collective Action* (Geneva: WHO, 2004).
6 UNIDO Evaluation Group, "Strengthening the local production of essential generic drugs in least developed/developing countries" (Vienna: UNIDO, 2011).
7 ITU, *Measuring the Information Society Report 2010* (Geneva: ITU, 2011).
8 ITU, www.itu.int/ict/statistics.
9 UNIDO's *Industrial Development Report 2009* quotes the British economist, Alfred Marshall's *Principles of Economics* (London: Macmillan, 1920).
10 Michael E. Porter, *The Competitive Advantage of Nations* (New York: Free Press, 1990).
11 UNIDO, *Industrial Development Report 2009* (Vienna: UNIDO, 2009), 33–34. There were a number of special factors that assisted the growth of Qiaotou, including strong institutional support from the provincial government and a major Italian investment to out-source button production.
12 UNIDO, "Cluster Development for Pro-poor Growth: the UNIDO Approach," Technical Paper Series (Vienna: UNIDO, 2010).
13 Traceability is a process of ensuring the safety and quality of food products at every stage from production through processing to delivery, as a means of facilitating the possible origins of contamination.
14 UNIDO, *Agro-Value Chain Analysis and Development* (Vienna: UNIDO, 2009).
15 Alain de Janvry, "Agriculture for Development—Implications for Agro-Industries," in *Agro-Industries for Development*, ed. Carlos A. da Silva *et al.* (Wallingford, Oxford: CAB International and FAO, 2009), 252.
16 Patrick Kormawa, "Agribusiness: Africa's Way Out of Poverty," *Making It*, 2nd quarter 2001 (Vienna: UNIDO, 2011): 18–21.
17 See Kandeh K. Yumkella, *Agribusiness for Africa's Prosperity* (Vienna: UNIDO, 2011), 53–55.
18 Patrick Kormawa, "Agribusiness: Africa's Way Out of Poverty," 18–23.
19 These manuals and guidelines can be found and accessed through the UNIDO website, www.unido.org/index.php?id=o3670.
20 UNIDO, "Independent Evaluation of COMFAR Activities" (Vienna: UNIDO, October 2010), www.unido.org/fileadmin/user_media/About_UNIDO/Evaluation/Project_reports/Comfar.PDF.
21 UNIDO Evaluation Group, *What has UNIDO done to reduce poverty?—Evidence from UNIDO evaluations 2008 and 2009* (Vienna: UNIDO, 2010).
22 OECD/DAC, *Poverty Reduction, The DAC Guidelines* (Paris: OECD, 2001).

5 Penetrating global markets

1 Preamble to the WTO *Agreement on the Application of Sanitary and Phytosanitary Measures* (SPS Agreement), www.wto.org/english/tratop_e/sps_e/spsagr_e.htm.
2 See Bernard M. Hoekman and Petros C. Mavroidis, *The World Trade Organization: Law, economics, and politics* (London: Routledge, 2007), 46.
3 UNIDO, *Meeting Standards, Winning Markets: Trade Standards Compliance 2010* (Vienna: UNIDO, 2011).
4 ISO and UNIDO, *Building Trust: the Conformity Assessment Toolbox* (Geneva: ISO, 2010).

140 *Notes*

5 UNIDO, "UNIDO Activities in the Area of Standards, Metrology, Testing and Quality," Thematic Evaluation Report (Vienna: UNIDO Evaluation Group, 2010).
6 WTO Aid for Trade Task Force, "Recommendations of the Task Force on Aid for Trade," WTO document WT/AFT/W/1 (Geneva: WTO, 2006).
7 UN, *Trade Capacity Building Resource Guide* (Vienna: UNIDO, 2010), www.unido.org/index.php?id=o86537.
8 The *Resource Guide* was produced under the auspices of the High-Level Committee on Programmes of the UN Chief Executives' Board.
9 These are global advocacy, trade policy development, legal and regulatory frameworks, supply capacity, compliance support infrastructure services, and market and trade information.

6 Greening industry

1 Paul Crutzen, Frank Sherwood Rowland and Mario Molina, who were later awarded the 1995 Nobel Prize in Chemistry.
2 For more details on the MLF, see Elizabeth R. DeSombre, *Global Environmental Institutions* (London: Routledge, 2006), 113–17.
3 In China it is over 70 percent according to the UNIDO Director in Beijing.
4 From 2001 to 2010 UNIDO was ranked as the best-performing of the four implementing agencies in eight out of the 10 years.
5 UNIDO, "Review to Extract Lessons from UNIDO Montreal Protocol Projects" (Vienna: UNIDO, 2010).
6 For more information on the background and workings of the Stockholm Convention, see Elizabeth R. DeSombre, *Global Environmental Institutions* (London: Routledge, 2006), 147–51.
7 Aldrin, Chlordane, Dichlorodiphenyltrichloroethane (DDT), Dieldrin, Dioxins, Endrin, Furans, Hexachlorobenzene, Heptachlor, Mirex, Polychlorinated biphenyls (PCBs) and Toxaphene.
8 The best-known is DDT, for which the inventor (Paul Hermann Muller of Switzerland) earned a Nobel Prize. It has subsequently been banned in most countries.
9 Stockholm Convention, chm.pops.int/Convention/tabid/54/language/en-US/Default.aspx#LiveContent[convtext].
10 See www.chemicalleasing.com for more information on the concept and the practical applications.
11 UNEP, *Government Strategies and Policies for Cleaner Production* (Paris: United Nations Environment Programme, 1994), 32.
12 UNIDO, "Taking Stock and Moving Forward: the UNIDO-UNEP National Cleaner Production Centres" (Vienna: UNIDO, 2010), 5–6.
13 UNIDO, "Independent Evaluation of the UNIDO-UNEO Cleaner Production Programme" (Vienna: UNIDO, May 2008), www.unido.org/fileadmin/user_media/About_UNIDO/Evaluation/CP_Program_Evaluation_Report_May_2008.pdf.
14 UNIDO, *Renewable Energy in Industrial Applications: An Assessment of the 2050 Potential* (Vienna: UNIDO, 2010).
15 IEA website, www.ruralelec.org/9.0.html.
16 UNIDO, "Independent Thematic Review: UNIDO Projects for the Promotion of Small Hydro Power for Productive Use" (Vienna: UNIDO, 2010), www.

Notes 141

unido.org/fileadmin/user_media/About_UNIDO/Evaluation/Project_reports/e-book_small-hydro.PDF.
17 M.W. Rosegrant, "Biofuels and grain prices: impacts and policy responses" (Washington, DC: International Food Policy Research Institute, May 2008).
18 Another major reason for the shortages was the growing global consumption of meat and dairy products, for which maize is a key feedstock.
19 UNIDO, "Navigating Bio-energy: Contributing to Informed Decision Making on Bio-energy Issues" (Vienna: UNIDO, 2009).
20 The location was chosen presumably because the United Arab Emirates (UAE) made the highest bid, notwithstanding the fact that it is an oil-rich country.

7 Facing the future

1 See Craig N. Murphy and JoAnne Yates, *The International Organization for Standardization (ISO): Global Governance through Voluntary Consensus* (London: Routledge, 2009).
2 UNIDO Evaluation Group, "UNIDO Activities in the area of Standards, Metrology, Testing and Quality," Thematic Evaluation Report (Vienna: UNIDO Evaluation Group, 2010). Another recent evaluation stated that "UNIDO programme/project managers view themselves as constrained by donor agendas, and thus not in a position to put themselves in the driver's seat" (UNIDO Evaluation Group, "What has UNIDO done to reduce poverty?—Evidence from UNIDO evaluations 2008 and 2009" (Vienna: UNIDO, 2010), xi.
3 UNIDO Evaluation Group, "UNIDO Integrated Programmes: Meta evaluation" (Vienna: UNIDO, 2010), 16.
4 UNIDO and Leuven Centre for Global Governance Studies, *Networks for Prosperity: Achieving Development Goals through Knowledge-Sharing* (Vienna: UNIDO, 2011), 27.
5 Industrial Development Board, Decision IDB.39/Dec.7 Programme and budgets, 2012–2013, 24 June 2011.

Select bibliography

Books

Several books have been written about UNIDO, usually giving the insiders' angle. For its 30-year anniversary, the organization itself published *United Nations Industrial Development Organization: 30 Years of Industrial Development 1966–1996* (London: International Systems and Communications, 1995), which contained articles by former directors-general about the early days. Within the last dozen years, two further books were written by a previous director-general, Carlos A. Magariños, about the challenges facing the organization during his term: *Reforming the UN System: UNIDO's Need-driven Model* (The Hague: Kluwer Law International, 2001) and *Economic Development and UN Reform: Towards a Common Agenda for Action* (Vienna: UNIDO, 2005). Another book that provides useful information on the organization's activities is Ralf Bredel's *Long-Term Conflict Prevention and Industrial Development: the United Nations and its Specialized Agency UNIDO* (Leiden, Netherlands: Martinus Nijhoff, 2003).

During the 1990s, when UNIDO faced its most important crises, two studies were commissioned by the Danish Ministry of Foreign Affairs to examine UNIDO's role and make recommendations about its future. The first, in 1992, was undertaken by COWIconsult and entitled "A Future UNIDO" (Copenhagen: DANIDA, Ministry of Foreign Affairs, 1992). Five years later, a team led by Professor John D. Martinussen of Roskilde University, Denmark, published *Assessment of UNIDO: Capacity Development for Sustainable Industrial Development Under Changed Conditions* (Copenhagen: Danish Ministry of Foreign Affairs, 1997). This latter report was partial inspiration for the *business plan* of the same year which laid the foundations for continuing reform.

There is an extensive literature on industrial development dating back to the 1960s. One of the pioneering thinkers on the subject was

Sanjaya Lall, who was closely associated with UNIDO and other UN organizations. Among other works, he wrote for UNIDO *The Growth of the Pharmaceutical Industry in Developing Countries* (Vienna: UNIDO, 1979). He also collaborated on UNIDO's *Industrial Development Reports* (IDRs), particularly the 2004 edition entitled *Industrialization, Environment and the Millennium Development Goals in Sub-Saharan Africa* (Vienna: UNIDO, 2004), which provides indicators of industrial competitiveness and assesses the main factors affecting it. A recent IDR was co-authored by Paul Collier and John Page: *Breaking In and Moving Up: New Industrial Challenges for the Bottom Billion and the Middle-Income Countries* (Vienna: UNIDO, 2009), which gives special attention to the countries that have been left behind in the industrialization process. Other IDRs in recent years are *Capacity Building for Catching-up: Historical, Empirical and Policy Dimensions* (Vienna: UNIDO, 2005), which draws lessons for industrialization from historical experience, and *Competing Through Innovation and Learning* (Vienna: UNIDO, 2002), which analyzes how sub-Saharan African countries could take advantage of environmentally sound and advanced technologies to advance their industrialization. A recent book, published by the UN, and which includes chapters by several noted authors is *Industrial Development for the 21st Century: Sustainable Development Perspectives* (New York: UN Department of Economic and Social Affairs, 2007).

Another rich bibliographical area is around industrial policy, a key theme for UNIDO. The subject has often been controversial, and ideologically based, being centered on the role of the state in development. Successful industrialization in East Asia, commencing with Japan, attracted attention to that country's approach to industrial policy. Chalmers A. Johnson's book, *MITI and the Japanese Miracle: The Growth of Industrial Policy, 1925–75* (Stanford University Press, 1982) is an example. More recently, Sanjaya Lall wrote *Learning from the Asian Tigers: Studies in Technology and Industrial Policy* (London: Macmillan, 1996). Lall also wrote "Reinventing Industrial Strategy: The Role of Government Policy in Building Institutional Competitiveness," G-24 Discussion Paper Series No. 28 (Geneva: UNCTAD, 2004). Ha-Joon Chang also drew on Asian experience in his *The East Asian Development Experience: The Miracle, the Crisis and the Future* (London: Zed Books, 2006), which discusses investment, trade and industrial policies. Chang also contributed an article to UNIDO's *Making It* magazine ("Towards a More Productive Debate," Issue 3, 2010), in which he puts the case for a wider acceptance of industrial policy. A more general work is Mario Cimoli, Giovanni Dosi and Joseph E. Stiglitz, *Industrial*

144 *Select bibliography*

Policy and Development: The Political Economy of Capabilities Accumulation (Oxford University Press, 2009). One of the most prolific authors on the subject is the Harvard academic, Dani Rodrik. For UNIDO, he wrote a paper in 2004, "Industrial Policy for the Twenty-First Century" (Cambridge, Mass.: UNIDO, 2004), and his "Normalizing Industrial Policy" (Cambridge, Mass., 2007) was prepared for the Commission on Growth and Development. In 2010 his online contributions included "The Return of Industrial Policy," Project Syndicate, 2010, www.project-syndicate.org/commentary/rodrik42/English.

On competitiveness there are also many useful sources, many of them inspired by Michael E. Porter's *The Competitive Advantage of Nations* (New York: Free Press, 1990), which defined competitiveness of countries and enterprises, based on value-chain analysis, and highlighted the importance of enterprise clustering. These ideas have been further refined by others and still provide inspiration for a lot of UNIDO's current work. Another academic who wrote widely on the subject was again Sanjaya Lall, who provided conceptual guidance to UNIDO and other UN agencies in this area. His writing included *Promoting Industrial Competitiveness in Developing Countries: Lessons from Asia*, Economic Paper No. 39 (London: Commonwealth Secretariat, 1999), *Building Industrial Competitiveness in Developing Countries* (Paris: OECD, 1990), and *Competitiveness, Technology and Skills* (Cheltenham: Edward Elgar, 2001).

On agro-industry, two of the best recent sources are from UNIDO itself: Carlos A. da Silva *et al.*, eds., *Agro-Industries for Development* (Wallingford, UK: CAB International with FAO and UNIDO, 2009), and Kandeh K. Yumkella, ed., *Agribusiness for Africa's Prosperity* (Vienna: UNIDO, 2011). Both these books benefit from the contributions of many experts and they put a forceful case for Africa, and low-income countries in other regions, to aggressively pursue the manufacture and processing of agricultural products as a basis for their development.

Sources on the environment and energy are numerous. In the context of this book, UNEP's *Government Strategies and Policies for Cleaner Production* (Paris: United Nations Environment Programme, 1994) is a key basic reference on the huge cleaner production campaign that will be required to reduce the environmental stress resulting from the industrialization process. A good introduction to the main global environmental organizations, conventions and funds (including the Montreal Protocol and its multilateral fund and the Global Environment Facility) is in Elizabeth R. DeSombre, *Global Environmental Institutions* (London: Routledge, 2006). Recently, UNIDO has also produced *Renewable*

Energy in Industrial Applications: An Assessment of the 2050 Potential (Vienna: 2010) as a guide to rendering industry more sustainable through the use of alternative energy sources.

Finally, on standards, a good reference is the book by Craig N. Murphy and JoAnne Yates, *The Industrial Organization for Standardization (ISO): Global Governance through Voluntary Consensus* (London: Routledge, 2009), which provides important background information on the organization, describes its unique method of working and the various standards that it has helped to develop, many of which are relevant to UNIDO's work. UNIDO has also produced a useful recent book that describes the complexity and importance of standards: UNIDO, *Meeting Standards, Winning Markets: Trade Standards Compliance 2010* (Vienna: UNIDO, 2011). UNIDO and ISO have also jointly published *Fast Forward: National Standards Bodies in Developing Countries* (Geneva: ISO and UNIDO, 2008), an introductory manual on creating or upgrading a national standards body, and *Building Trust: the Conformity Assessment Toolbox* (Geneva: ISO and UNIDO, 2010), a handbook on all aspects of conformity assessment and its role in international trade.

Websites

UNIDO's own website, www.unido.org, is low-key but friendly and navigable. It gives access to a substantial number of documents, both promotional and substantive, as well as video-clips. A strong feature of the site (and the organization) is the long list of evaluation reports, which are objective and informative. Other websites that provide information relevant to aspects of UNIDO's work include the International Organization for Standardization (www.iso.org) and the UN Environment Programme (www.unep.org).

Index

Abdel-Rahman, Ibrahim Helmi 28
Abu Dhabi 123
Abuja Declaration 78
Afghanistan 23, 36, 79
African Agribusiness and
  Agro-industries Development
  Initiative (3ADI) 78–79
Africa Investment Promotion
  Agency Network (AfrIPANet) 84
Agenda 21 107
agri-business 59, 73–79
agro-processing 59, 73–79
Aid for Trade (AfT) 8, 40, 89,
  96–98
Algeria 28, 36, 65, 67
Annan, Kofi 102
Armenia 36, 110
Australia 19, 28
Austria 15, 29, 41, 43

Bahrain 37, 38, 80, 131
Bangladesh 36
Belgium 37, 41, 80
Bhutan 64
bio-energy 120–21
Bolivia 36
Botswana 3, 56
Brazil 36, 62, 65, 67, 74, 92, 121
Brazil, Russian Federation, India,
  China, South Africa (BRICS) 62
Bretton Woods institutions (BWIs)
  see World Bank, International
  Monetary Fund
Burkina Faso 36, 77
Burundi 94
business environment 79–80

business information centers (BIC)
  66, 118

Cambodia 36
Cameroon 18, 36, 39, 50–51, 93
Canada 19, 28, 43
Cape Verde 51, 120
chemical leasing (ChL) 106
Chevron 41
China 3, 36, 37, 38, 42, 50, 62, 64,
  67, 80, 107, 108, 115, 116, 117,
  119, 131
  TVE Township and village
    enterprises 3
chlorofluorocarbon (CFC) 7, 101–4
Civil Society Organizations (CSOs) 46
climate change 7, 33, 40, 100–101,
  111, 113–14
clustering 67–70
Cluster Development Agent (CDA)
  68–70
cleaner production 107–13
Cold War 17
Colombia 36, 50, 108
Commission on Global Governance
  18, 28
Congo, Democratic Republic 36
corporate social responsibility 62
Côte d'Ivoire 36, 40, 63
country ownership 54
creative industries 64
Croatia 104, 110
Cuba 119–20

DDT (Dichlorodiphenyltrichloroethane) 105

decoupling 112–13
Denmark 18, 20–21, 58, 119, 142
Doha Round 96–97

East Asian industrialization 2–4
East African Community 94
Economic Community of West African States (ECOWAS) 120
Centre for Renewable Energy and Energy Efficiency (ECREE) 120
Ecuador 36, 50
Egypt 3, 28, 36, 41, 64, 67, 72–73, 106
Enhanced Integrated Framework for Least Developed Countries (EIF) 40, 44, 97
Eritrea 36, 63
Essential drugs 64–65
Ethiopia 36, 69–70
European Commission (EC) 35, 43–44, 98, 122
European Union (EU) 6, 91, 110
Export consortia 72–73

Fairtrade 90
Finland 41
Food and Agriculture Organization (of the UN) (FAO) 24, 31, 35, 40, 78, 97, 125, 144
foreign direct investment (FDI) 2, 3, 60, 62, 70, 79–80, 85, 89
France 37, 43, 80
Future of the UN Development System (FUNDS) Project xii

G77 developing countries 13, 127
Gambia 51
General Agreement on Tariffs and Trade (GATT) 13
Germany 17, 19–20, 43, 72–73, 123
Ghana 36, 84
Global Environment Facility (GEF) 40, 44, 105–6, 120
globalization 4, 6, 59, 67, 75, 98, 131
Good manufacturing practice (GMP) 65
green industry 7–8, 26, 100–124
Gross domestic product (GDP) and manufacturing 1–3, 49, 55, 74, 113
Guatemala 110

Guinea 36, 40, 63, 106
Guinea Current Large Marine Ecosystem (GCLME) 106

hydrochlorofluorocarbon (HCFC) 101–4
HIV/AIDS 64, 78
Heritage Foundation 21
Hewlett-Packard 41, 66–67
Hong Kong 2–3, 50
Hong Kong Ministerial Meeting of the WTO 97
hydrogen technology 122

India 3, 10, 36, 42, 43, 62, 67, 69, 71, 78, 96, 107, 117, 119, 121
Indonesia 2, 23, 36, 117, 121
information (and communication) technology 4, 41, 42, 65–66, 76
industrial policy debate 5–7, 51–56
International Accreditation Forum (IAF) 95
International Atomic Energy Agency (IAEA) 126
International Centre for Hydrogen Energy Technologies (ICHET) 42, 122
International Centre for the Promotion and Transfer of Solar Energy (ISEC, China) 119
International Centres for Small Hydropower (China, India, Nigeria) 42, 117
International Centre for Science and High Technology (Trieste) 85
International Civil Aviation Organization (ICAO) 125
International Development Association (see World Bank)
International Energy Agency (IEA) 115, 116, 122
International Finance Corporation (see World Bank)
International Fund for Agricultural Development (IFAD) 40, 78, 126
International Laboratory Accreditation Cooperation (ILAC) 95
International Labour Organization (ILO) 40, 56, 63

148 *Index*

International Maritime Organization (IMO) 125
International Monetary Fund (IMF) xi, 5, 13,
International Network for Educational Exchange (INEX)
International Organization for Standardization (ISO) 90, 92, 95, 110, 115, 125, 131, 145
International Renewable Energy Agency (IRENA) 123
International Telecommunication Union (ITU) 65, 92, 125
International Trade Centre (ITC) 25–26, 31, 40, 97
investment promotion 79–84
Investment and Technology Promotion Office (ITPO) (see UNIDO)
Investment Promotion Agency (IPA) 83–84
Iran 36
Italy 22, 37, 41, 43, 80, 85
Iraq 23–24, 44–45, 56

Japan 2, 20, 29, 36, 43, 80, 143
Jordan 36, 65

Kenya 36, 63, 67, 94, 110, 111, 118
Khane, Abd-El Rahman 28
Kuznets, Simon 10
Kyoto Protocol 104
Kyrgyzstan 36

Laos 24, 36
Least Developed Countries (LDCs) 59, 65, 74, 93–94, 97
Least developed manufacturing countries 4–5
Lebanon 36, 41, 45
Lewis, W. Arthur 10
Liberia 63

Macedonia 104
Madagascar 36, 77
Magariños, Carlos A. 21, 25, 28, 29, 142
Mali 36, 77
manufacturing value added (MVA) 1, 3

Malaysia 2,-3, 50, 116
Mano River Union 63
Maria y Campos, Mauricio de 27, 29
mercury 105
methyl bromide 101, 102, 103
metrology 94–95
Mexico 29, 36, 37, 80
micro and small enterprises (MSE) 63, 65
Microsoft 66
Millennium Declaration 25
Millennium Development Goal (MDG) 27, 44, 45, 48, 58, 65, 86, 123
Millennium Cities Initiative 70
Mongolia 48, 55–56, 95
Montenegro 39
Montreal Protocol 7–8, 17, 25, 33, 40, 44, 100–104, 122, 127
Multilateral Fund 101–4
Morocco 36, 41, 63, 67, 72, 106
Mozambique 36, 94, 118
Multilateral Mutual Recognition Agreement (MLA) 95
Mutual Recognition Agreement (MRA) 95

National Cleaner Production Centers (NCPCs) (see UNIDO)
national implementation plans 104
national metrology institutes 94–95
national standards bodies 92–94
Nepal 93–94
Netherlands 41
New international economic order (NIEO) 13, 14, 21, 46, 57, 127
Nicaragua 36, 69–70
Nigeria 25, 29, 36, 42, 43, 67, 78, 84, 117
non-governmental organizations (NGOs) xi, 40, 90, 125
Norway 43

ozone-depleting substances 7, 101–4, 122
Organization of Black Sea Cooperation 122
Organisation for Economic Co-operation and Development (OECD) 17, 47, 97, 144

Development Assistance Committee (DAC) 86–87
Office for Project Execution (OPE) 16
Organization of Petroleum-Exporting Countries (OPEC) 12, 14

Pakistan 36
Palestine 51, 65
Paraguay 50
persistent organic pollutants (POPs) 40, 100, 104–5
Peru 13, 39, 111
Philippines 36
photo-voltaic systems 118–19
Porter, Michael E. 67
poverty reduction 8, 23, 24, 25, 26, 31, 32, 40, 57, 58–59, 65, 68, 69, 73, 79, 86–87, 129
private sector development 52–53, 56, 62–63

quality standards 89–96
private standards 90–91
renewable energy 113–24

Resource efficient and cleaner production (RECP) (see UNIDO)
Rio Summits 107, 127
Rodrik, Daniel 6, 53–54, 144
Robertson, Dennis 10
rural electrification 116–20
Russian Federation 37, 43, 80, 110
Rwanda 36, 51, 94, 117

Samoa 39
Saudi Arabia 67
science, technology and innovation (STI) 75
Senegal 36, 77
Siazon, Domingo L. 15, 27, 29
Sierra Leone 29, 36, 40, 63, 118
Singapore 2, 49, 52
Singer, Hans 10
Slovakia 110
small and medium-sized enterprises (SMEs) 41, 63, 65–66, 69–72, 76, 80, 83, 108, 113, 114
small hydro-power 42, 116–17

SMTQ (standards, metrology, testing and quality) 96
solar energy 118–19
South Africa 36, 65, 67, 74, 109
South-South cooperation 31, 42, 62, 75, 96, 117, 131
South Korea 2, 37, 80
South Sudan 63
SPS (Sanitary and Phyto-Sanitary) agreement 40, 88–89, 94, 97
Sri Lanka 108, 111, 117
Standards and Trade Development Facility (STDF) 40, 97
Stockholm Convention 100, 104–5
Strategic Approach to International Chemical Management (SAICM) 105
Sudan 23, 36, 63
supply-chains 69–71, 91
Switzerland 37, 43
Syria 41

Taiwan (Chinese Taipei) 2,
Tanzania 36, 63, 77, 84, 94
TBT (Technical Barriers to Trade) agreement 88–89, 94
technical assistance, technical cooperation 7–8, 9, 12, 16–17, 25–26, 42, 62, 107
technology promotion 84–86
Thailand 2, 3, 36, 50, 74, 116
Tinbergen, Jan 10
trade 4–5, 26, 88–99, 128
trade capacity building 88–99, 128
Trade-Related Intellectual Property Rights (TRIPS) agreement 64
Transfer of Environmentally Sound Technology (TEST) (see UNIDO)
transnational corporations (TNCs) 62
Tunisia 3, 36, 41, 67, 106
Turkey 36, 122
Tuvalu 39

Uganda 23, 36, 41, 66, 67, 77, 84, 94
United Arab Emirates 67
United Kingdom 19–20, 26–27, 29, 37, 45, 80, 107, 127
Department for International Development (DfID) 26–27

150 *Index*

United Nations
  Delivering as One (DAO) 32; Economic and Social Council (ECOSOC) 10–11; General Assembly 11, 13, 27; Global Compact 62; High-Level Group on Sustainable Energy for All 25, 28, 40, 123; High-Level Panel on System-wide Coherence 39; International Year of Sustainable Energy for All 123–24; Secretary-General 12, 14, 22, 25, 39, 102; UN Development Assistance Framework (UNDAF) 40; UN-ENERGY 25, 39, 100, 123–24; UN System Chief Executives Board for Coordination (CEB) 25
UN Centre on Transnational Corporations (UNCTC) 62
United Nations Children's Fund (UNICEF) 126
United Nations Conference on Trade and Development (UNCTAD) 11, 13, 14, 18, 19, 25–26, 31, 40, 62, 97, 126, 127, 143
United Nations Development Programme (UNDP) 11, 16, 30, 40, 97, 102–3, 126
  As coordinator 16; as funder of UNIDO 16–17, 43–44; *Human Development Report* 58; joint offices with UNIDO 30, 35, 39
United Nations Economic Commission for Africa (UNECA) 97
United Nations Educational, Scientific and Cultural Organization (UNESCO) 126
United Nations Environment Programme (UNEP) 31, 40, 102, 103, 104, 105, 107, 109, 112, 119, 126, 144
United Nations Foundation 124
United Nations High Commissioner for Refugees (UNHCR) 126
United Nations Industrial Development Organization (UNIDO)
  business plan 20–22; combating marginalization and poverty through industrial development (COMPID) 58–59; Competitive industrial performance (CIP) index 49–50; Computer Model for Feasibility Analysis and Reporting (COMFAR) 81–82; criticism by developed countries 9, 15, 18–19, 26, 51–52, 126–27; evaluations 23–24, 34–35, 38, 65, 81, 86, 95–96, 104, 111, 117, 130; field offices 22, 30, 35–38; funding concerns 12, 15–17, 19, 42–45; general conferences 13, 14, 18, 27, 38–39; global forum role 8, 13, 46, 76, 115, 127; governance 38–39; Industrial Development Board 11, 39; Industrial Development Fund 17, 43–44; integrated programs 23, 35; *Industrial Development Reports* 47, 48, 50; investment promotion 22; Investment and Technology Promotion Office (ITPO) 22, 30, 34, 35, 38, 60, 80–81, 131; investment appraisal tools 81–82; investor surveys 82; Learning Initiative for Entrepreneurs (LIFE) 67; *Lima Declaration* 13, 27; *Making It* 5; objectives 14–15; mission statement 31–32, 59; National Cleaner Production Centers (NCPCs) 106, 107–12, 131; partnerships 7–8, 27, 39–41, 45, 47, 62, 115, 130–31; post-conflict programs 23–24; Program Approval Committee 34; Program Approval and Monitoring Committee (AMC) 34; Program for Change and Organizational Renewal 31; reforms 18–23, 25, 27, 32–35; Resource Efficient and Cleaner Production (RECP) program 112, 131; *Resource Guide in Trade Capacity Building* 98; results-based management 25; Senior Industrial Development Field Advisor 35; *Solving the E-waste Problem (StEP)* 107;

Index 151

specialized agency status 15; staffing 16, 25, 34, 129; structure 33–34; *Subcontracting and Partnership Exchange Programme (SPX)* 83–84; thematic priorities 23, 26, 31, 33, 59, 127–29; *Transfer of Environmentally Sound Technology (TEST)* 106; *UNIDO Centre for South-South Industrial Cooperation (UCSSIC, New Delhi)* 42, 96; University Chair on Innovation (UNCHAIN) 41; *World Statistics on Mining and Utilities* 48; Yaoundé Conference 18; *Yearbook of Industrial Statistics* 47–48; Young Professionals Program 25
UN Office for Drugs and Crime (UNODC) 23
United Nations Population Fund (UNFPA) 126
United Nations University (UNU) 41
  UNU-MERIT (Maastricht Economic and Social Research Institute of Innovation and Technology) 41
  UNU-WIDER (World Institute for Development Economics Research) 41
United States 19, 37, 119
Universal Postal Union 125
University of Ghent 41
University of Oxford 41

Uruguay 36, 56, 105
Uruguay Round 89

value-chains 23, 60–61, 67–69, 75, 79, 88, 129
Vienna 123
Vienna International Centre 11, 15–16, 27, 28, 29, 34, 39, 41
Vienna Convention 7, 100–101
Vietnam 36, 51, 79–80, 82, 86, 108

Ward, Barbara 10
Washington consensus 5
wind energy 119–20
World Food Programme (WFP) 126
World Health Organization (WHO) 65, 97, 126
World Bank xi, 5, 10, 13, 25, 56, 97, 102
  International Finance Corporation 63
World Meteorological Organization (WMO) 126
World Organization for Animal Health 97
World Trade Organization (WTO) xi, 40, 44, 64, 88, 89, 93, 94, 96, 97, 98

Yugoslavia 10
Yumkella, Kandeh 25, 27, 28, 29, 73, 144

Zambia 43
Zimbabwe 36, 63, 74

Routledge Global Institutions Series

66 United Nations Industrial Development Organization (2012)
by Stephen Browne (FUNDS Project)

65 The Millennium Development Goals and Beyond (2012)
Global development after 2015
edited by Rorden Wilkinson (University of Manchester) and David Hulme (University of Manchester)

64 International Organizations as Self-Directed Actors (2012)
A framework for analysis
edited by Joel E. Oestreich (Drexel University)

63 Maritime Piracy (2012)
by Robert Haywood and Roberta Spivak

62 United Nations High Commissioner for Refugees (UNHCR) (2nd edition, 2012)
by Gil Loescher (University of Oxford), Alexander Betts (University of Oxford), and James Milner (University of Toronto)

61 International Law, International Relations, and Global Governance (2012)
by Charlotte Ku (University of Illinois)

60 Global Health Governance (2012)
by Sophie Harman (City University, London)

59 The Council of Europe (2012)
by Martyn Bond (University of London)

58 The Security Governance of Regional Organizations (2011)
edited by Emil J. Kirchner (University of Essex) and Roberto Domínguez (Suffolk University)

57 The United Nations Development Programme and System (2011)
by Stephen Browne (FUNDS Project)

56 The South Asian Association for Regional Cooperation (2011)
An emerging collaboration architecture
by Lawrence Sáez (University of London)

55 The UN Human Rights Council (2011)
by Bertrand G. Ramcharan (Geneva Graduate Institute of International and Development Studies)

54 The Responsibility to Protect (2011)
Cultural perspectives in the Global South
edited by Rama Mani (University of Oxford) and Thomas G. Weiss (The CUNY Graduate Center)

53 The International Trade Centre (2011)
Promoting exports for development
by Stephen Browne (FUNDS Project) and Sam Laird (University of Nottingham)

52 The Idea of World Government (2011)
From ancient times to the twenty-first century
by James A. Yunker (Western Illinois University)

51 Humanitarianism Contested (2011)
Where angels fear to tread
by Michael Barnett (George Washington University) and Thomas G. Weiss (The CUNY Graduate Center)

50 The Organization of American States (2011)
Global governance away from the media
by Monica Herz (Catholic University, Rio de Janeiro)

49 Non-Governmental Organizations in World Politics (2011)
The construction of global governance
by Peter Willetts (City University, London)

48 The Forum on China-Africa Cooperation (FOCAC) (2011)
by Ian Taylor (University of St. Andrews)

47 Global Think Tanks (2011)
Policy networks and governance
by James G. McGann (University of Pennsylvania) with Richard Sabatini

46 United Nations Educational, Scientific and Cultural Organization (UNESCO) (2011)
Creating norms for a complex world
by J.P. Singh (Georgetown University)

45 The International Labour Organization (2011)
Coming in from the cold
by Steve Hughes (Newcastle University) and Nigel Haworth (University of Auckland)

44 Global Poverty (2010)
How global governance is failing the poor
by David Hulme (University of Manchester)

43 Global Governance, Poverty, and Inequality (2010)
edited by Jennifer Clapp (University of Waterloo) and Rorden Wilkinson (University of Manchester)

42 Multilateral Counter-Terrorism (2010)
by Peter Romaniuk (John Jay College of Criminal Justice, CUNY)

41 Governing Climate Change (2010)
by Peter Newell (University of East Anglia) and Harriet A. Bulkeley (Durham University)

40 The UN Secretary-General and Secretariat (2nd edition, 2010)
by Leon Gordenker (Princeton University)

39 Preventive Human Rights Strategies (2010)
by Bertrand G. Ramcharan (Geneva Graduate Institute of International and Development Studies)

38 African Economic Institutions (2010)
by Kwame Akonor (Seton Hall University)

37 Global Institutions and the HIV/AIDS Epidemic (2010)
Responding to an international crisis
by Franklyn Lisk (University of Warwick)

36 Regional Security (2010)
The capacity of international organizations
by Rodrigo Tavares (United Nations University)

35 The Organisation for Economic Co-operation and Development (2009)
by Richard Woodward (University of Hull)

34 Transnational Organized Crime (2009)
by Frank Madsen (University of Cambridge)

33 The United Nations and Human Rights (2nd edition, 2009)
A guide for a new era
by Julie A. Mertus (American University)

32 The International Organization for Standardization (2009)
Global governance through voluntary consensus
by Craig N. Murphy (Wellesley College) and JoAnne Yates (Massachusetts Institute of Technology)

31 Shaping the Humanitarian World (2009)
by Peter Walker (Tufts University) and Daniel G. Maxwell (Tufts University)

30 Global Food and Agricultural Institutions (2009)
by John Shaw

29 Institutions of the Global South (2009)
by Jacqueline Anne Braveboy-Wagner (City College of New York, CUNY)

28 International Judicial Institutions (2009)
The architecture of international justice at home and abroad
by Richard J. Goldstone (Retired Justice of the Constitutional Court of South Africa) and Adam M. Smith (Harvard University)

27 The International Olympic Committee (2009)
The governance of the Olympic system
by Jean-Loup Chappelet (IDHEAP Swiss Graduate School of Public Administration) and Brenda Kübler-Mabbott

26 The World Health Organization (2009)
by Kelley Lee (London School of Hygiene and Tropical Medicine)

25 Internet Governance (2009)
The new frontier of global institutions
by John Mathiason (Syracuse University)

24 Institutions of the Asia-Pacific (2009)
ASEAN, APEC, and beyond
by Mark Beeson (University of Birmingham)

23 United Nations High Commissioner for Refugees (UNHCR) (2008)
The politics and practice of refugee protection into the twenty-first century
by Gil Loescher (University of Oxford), Alexander Betts (University of Oxford), and James Milner (University of Toronto)

22 Contemporary Human Rights Ideas (2008)
by Bertrand G. Ramcharan (Geneva Graduate Institute of International and Development Studies)

21 The World Bank (2008)
From reconstruction to development to equity
by Katherine Marshall (Georgetown University)

20 The European Union (2008)
by Clive Archer (Manchester Metropolitan University)

19 The African Union (2008)
Challenges of globalization, security, and governance
by Samuel M. Makinda (Murdoch University) and F. Wafula Okumu (McMaster University)

18 Commonwealth (2008)
Inter- and non-state contributions to global governance
by Timothy M. Shaw (Royal Roads University)

17 The World Trade Organization (2007)
Law, economics, and politics
by Bernard M. Hoekman (World Bank) and Petros C. Mavroidis (Columbia University)

16 A Crisis of Global Institutions? (2007)
Multilateralism and international security
by Edward Newman (University of Birmingham)

15 UN Conference on Trade and Development (2007)
by Ian Taylor (University of St. Andrews) and Karen Smith (University of Stellenbosch)

14 The Organization for Security and Co-operation in Europe (2007)
by David J. Galbreath (University of Aberdeen)

13 The International Committee of the Red Cross (2007)
A neutral humanitarian actor
by David P. Forsythe (University of Nebraska) and Barbara Ann Rieffer-Flanagan (Central Washington University)

12 **The World Economic Forum (2007)**
   A multi-stakeholder approach to global governance
   by Geoffrey Allen Pigman (Bennington College)

11 **The Group of 7/8 (2007)**
   by Hugo Dobson (University of Sheffield)

10 **The International Monetary Fund (2007)**
   Politics of conditional lending
   by James Raymond Vreeland (Georgetown University)

9 **The North Atlantic Treaty Organization (2007)**
   The enduring alliance
   by Julian Lindley-French (Center for Applied Policy, University of Munich)

8 **The World Intellectual Property Organization (2006)**
   Resurgence and the development agenda
   by Chris May (University of the West of England)

7 **The UN Security Council (2006)**
   Practice and promise
   by Edward C. Luck (Columbia University)

6 **Global Environmental Institutions (2006)**
   by Elizabeth R. DeSombre (Wellesley College)

5 **Internal Displacement (2006)**
   Conceptualization and its consequences
   by Thomas G. Weiss (The CUNY Graduate Center) and David A. Korn

4 **The UN General Assembly (2005)**
   by M.J. Peterson (University of Massachusetts, Amherst)

3 **United Nations Global Conferences (2005)**
   by Michael G. Schechter (Michigan State University)

2 **The UN Secretary-General and Secretariat (2005)**
   by Leon Gordenker (Princeton University)

1 **The United Nations and Human Rights (2005)**
   A guide for a new era
   by Julie A. Mertus (American University)

Books currently under contract include:

The Regional Development Banks
Lending with a regional flavor
by Jonathan R. Strand (University of Nevada)

Millennium Development Goals (MDGs)
For a people-centered development agenda?
by Sakiko Fukada-Parr (The New School)

Peacebuilding
From concept to commission
by Robert Jenkins (The CUNY Graduate Center)

Human Security
by Don Hubert (University of Ottawa)

UNICEF
by Richard Jolly (University of Sussex)

FIFA
by Alan Tomlinson (University of Brighton)

The Bank for International Settlements
The politics of global financial supervision in the age of high finance
by Kevin Ozgercin (SUNY College at Old Westbury)

International Migration
by Khalid Koser (Geneva Centre for Security Policy)

Human Development
by Richard Ponzio

Religious Institutions and Global Politics
by Katherine Marshall (Georgetown University)

The Group of Twenty (G20)
*by Andrew F. Cooper (Centre for International Governance Innovation, Ontario)
and Ramesh Thakur (Balsillie School of International Affairs, Ontario)*

The International Monetary Fund (2nd edition)
Politics of conditional lending
by James Raymond Vreeland (Georgetown University)

The UN Global Compact
by Catia Gregoratti (Lund University)

Institutions for Women's Rights
by Charlotte Patton (York College, CUNY) and Carolyn Stephenson (University of Hawaii)

International Aid
by Paul Mosley (University of Sheffield)

Global Consumer Policy
by Karsten Ronit (University of Copenhagen)

The Changing Political Map of Global Governance
by Anthony Payne (University of Sheffield) and Stephen Robert Buzdugan (Manchester Metropolitan University)

Coping with Nuclear Weapons
by W. Pal Sidhu

Global Sustainability
by Tapio Kanninen

Private Foundations and Development Partnerships
by Michael Moran (Swinburne University of Technology)

Decolonization, Sovereignty, and the African Union
by Martin Welz (University of Konstanz)

Feminist Strategies in International Governance
edited by Gülay Caglar (Humboldt University of Berlin), Elisabeth Prügl (Graduate Institute of International and Development Studies, Geneva), Susanne Zwingel (SUNY Potsdam)

For further information regarding the series, please contact:
Craig Fowlie, Senior Publisher, Politics & International Studies
Taylor & Francis
2 Park Square, Milton Park, Abingdon
Oxford OX14 4RN, UK
+44 (0)207 842 2057 Tel
+44 (0)207 842 2302 Fax
Craig.Fowlie@tandf.co.uk
www.routledge.com